OPENING MINDS
OPENING DOORS

OPENING MINDS

MINDS

The Rebirth of American Education

OPENING

DOORS

DAN HULL

CORD
COMMUNICATIONS

ISBN 1-55502-485-8
Library of Congress Number 93-072695

Printed in the United States of America

Grateful acknowledgment is made to:

the Cincinnati Post for reprint of the editorial cartoon "Evolution of A Career,"

Gene Bottoms, Alice Presson, Mary Johnson, and the Southern Regional Education Board for the reprint of the data table, "SREB Pilot Site Comparison of Student Achievement in Applied Mathematics Versus Traditional Mathematics Curriculum,"

Clark M. Greene, Manager of Training, at Georgetown Steel Corporation for the reprint of his letter addressed to the National Tech Prep Network,

Dr. William Halbert for his research and written contribution to chapter 9, and

Dr. Walt Edling for his research and written contribution to chapter 5.

CONTENTS

FOREWORD

Clearly it is time to change the way we do business in education. If recent trends continue, up to three-quarters of new employees will have insufficient verbal and writing skills by the year 2000, while technology will demand more high skilled jobs than we can currently provide. The nation is facing a monumental mismatch between jobs and the ability of Americans to do them. This growing interdependence between education and economics has made it more important than ever before to recognize the strong link between what students are asked to learn and what they will do with the rest of their lives.

We simply cannot expect to change our approach to education effectively without considering the fact that the workplace is changing and the demographics of our society are changing. Young students who are currently economically or socially disadvantaged will make up a large portion of tomorrow's workforce—we cannot forget these students. The future of American business depends on our greatest resource, our youth. And our youth depend on us to prepare them for a successful future in American business.

This means that we must prepare *all* students for a quality educational experience. One that goes beyond the abstract theories in the textbook or classroom to the practical uses and applications of education in careers and the workplace.

In Florida, we've been about making these types of changes in education for the last six years. The driving force behind Florida's Blueprint for Career Preparation has been a commitment that students graduating from Florida's public schools be prepared to begin a career *and* continue their education at a postsecondary technical school, community college, or university. We are working toward this goal in all grade levels (K-16) through career awareness, technological literacy, personal assessment, career exploration, academic and specific skill development, career advancement, and postsecondary education. All our efforts involve business/industry and the community to ensure an education that supports Florida's economy.

Our practices for a quality educational system reflect the vision that Dan Hull offers as the greatest opportunity for the rebirth of American education. He makes a convincing case for the argument that Tech Prep/Associate Degree is a viable agent for change in the public school system. He provides the answers for giving students the guidance and preparation they need without closing their options for continuing education beyond high school. *Opening Minds, Opening Doors* is also about putting education back into the laps of those who can make a difference—teachers. And its about empowering teachers to teach contextually, to use laboratories in and out of the classroom, to understand the workplace, and make learning useful and meaningful for the student who needs to know and understand the workplace. Our experience in Florida has shown that these concepts of Tech Prep work and they make a difference.

Betty Castor
Florida Commissioner of Education

PREFACE

For over thirty years, schools have not been particularly effective in preparing most students for life, for careers, or for further education. Yes, we have made sincere efforts to provide alternatives for non-baccalaureate-bound students. Agreed, we have strived to deal with the increasingly complex social problems surrounding these students. But in doing so we have neglected to provide a structured, purposeful education that deserves and requires all students' best efforts, a curriculum that expects and delivers high achievement by all. Consequently, an alarming number of students has left school ill-prepared either to embark on sustainable careers or to be productive members of America's workforce. In global terms, these students have suffered from a second-rate education while American businesses have suffered from the limitations of poorly equipped workers. As a result, the limited educational performance of so many of our students is posing a threat to us all—to our economy, to our standard of living, to our way of life.

But I am proud to say that it is not in this country's nature to accept second place in anything for very long. Out of the many and varied responses to this well-publicized educational crisis have emerged the dramatic vision and the proven components for an education that can equip the majority of today's students for new and exciting futures. This initiative is called Tech Prep/Associate Degree (Tech Prep for short), and it is quietly changing thousands of lives while changing the face of American schools. From coast to coast, Tech Prep is opening minds to a new way of doing the business of education while opening new career doors for our graduates through meaningful and useful learning experiences.

Tech Prep is a program that for the first time recognizes the unique learning and motivational needs of students, the changed and changing skill needs of employers, and the need for a new kind of integration of academic and occupational knowledge as preparation for a lifetime of learning. Tech Prep/Associate Degree is a significant educational reform that requires full and equal participation from high schools, community colleges, and employers to design, develop, and deliver an education that works. Coupling the four years of high school with two years at a community college—and including complementary work-based and work-site learning along with the always-present opportunity to continue to further degrees—Tech Prep keeps students interested and motivated to stay in school while empowering them for a meaningful role in America's society and workforce.

The vision of Tech Prep/Associate Degree that I have just described has been evolving over the past ten years, and in most places Tech Prep will continue to evolve for some time to come. The more than one thousand Tech Prep initiatives started in the United States are still developing—many of them have only recently left the planning stage—and have not matured into seasoned models of educational excellence.

I have written this book to describe the vision of this still largely unreported educational phenomenon. I have tried to illustrate the characteristics and promise of Tech Prep through many examples of extraordinary and varied collaborative efforts to bring it to practical reality. These are stories and successes that deserve the attention of high school and college administrators, faculty, and board members, as well as parents, policymakers, and business leaders interested in or concerned about the state of America's education. And along the way I have described and discussed two concepts that are fundamental to most successful Tech Prep programs: *contextual learning* (how most students learn best, and how they can best be taught) and *school-work integration* (through which we can restore education to its centrally relevant role as preparation for our lives, our careers, and our dreams).

Writing this book has been a thrilling and challenging experience. It has also been a major privilege as I have tried to do justice to the innovation, energy and cooperation of hundreds of dedicated educators and citizens who are the heart, arms and legs of Tech Prep. To all of these men and women, I express my sincere admiration and gratitude, along with the nostalgic regret that you were not a part of my own early education and that of my children.

A special "thank you" is offered to Drs. Maurice Dutton, Leno Pedrotti, and Steve Sadler and Mr. Piers Bateman for their helpful discussions and suggestions. I appreciate Dr. Walt Edling for his insightful work and contributions on curriculum integration in chapter 5 and Dr. William Halbert, who wrote most of the original manuscript for chapter 9. Thanks to the creativity of the editor Ann Christian Buchanan this book now has more clarity and meaning for the average reader.

Lastly, I want to thank my wife, Rita for her patience and Julie Vitale, my daughter (and experienced Tech Prep Coordinator) who unselfishly left the Gulf Coast Tech Prep Consortium in the fall of 1992 to help me write this book.

Dan Hull
August 1993

PART ONE

Catching the Tech Prep Vision

1.

AN OPEN DOOR TO

**The Promise and
Possibilities of
Tech Prep/
Associate Degree**

EDUCATIONAL EXCELLENCE

Do you know these people? Are they your students—your children—your future employees?

- *"I'm just dumb."* Sonya is frustrated with her school work and her seeming inability to achieve the grades that her peers achieve. She feels like a failure and has little confidence that she can be useful in any capacity. She tries not to think too much about her future.

- *"I don't have a chance."* Dwight, who lives in the inner city, feels trapped in his low-income community. He lacks the money, skills, and options for leaving the community and building a life and career outside his present environment.

- *"I've got other things on my mind."* Jessica loves everything about school except school! She has a passion for athletics, friends, and/or extracurricular activities but almost no interest in academics. Jessica's family has encouraged her to study and make good grades, but she has always maintained a low "C" average. She plans to attend a university but will leave after the second semester—either because her grades are not good enough or because she found another interest.

- *"I just want to be on my own."* Julio has always maintained high grades but has no real interest in attending a university. He is eager to begin a career and be independent, but he isn't sure how to make this possible.

- *"Who cares?"* Sam has never had any encouragement from his family or friends to make school a priority. Not surprisingly, he has little concept of how an education may help him attain a career. He's just marking time in school until he's old enough to drop out and go to work in his brother-in-law's body shop.

- *"Someday I'll be a star."* Becca sets unrealistic goals for herself to become an actress or doctor without the knowledge of how to attain these goals. She does not understand that other careers are available or realize that she may have other talents and interests.

These six teenagers represent the majority of students attending our nation's high schools. They also represent the future of America's workforce. And their chances of working productively and making a living in tomorrow's society are steadily decreasing—primarily because of an educational system that fails to address their educational needs and shuts a door on their future possibilities.

These kids may be economically or socially trapped, and most of them either are disinterested in academics or lack the confidence that they can succeed in school. Many have no interest in baccalaureate studies after high school; some don't even care if they finish high school. They don't see how what they're being asked to learn in school will ever matter in their life or their work.

These are the "forgotten half" (sometimes called the "neglected majority") of our high school students. Neither the top achievers nor the special needs kids, they are the average students that the American education system doesn't seem to care about. For the most part they have little direction, low expectations, and little hope of becoming all they can be.

We often make two assumptions about these students:

- They can't be motivated to learn.

- They don't really have the ability to handle academic subjects.

But the experience of educators and policymakers who have dared to take a different approach to education proves these assumptions wrong. The problem lies not so much in the attitudes and abilities of these students as in a system of education that essentially ignores them. And the answer is an approach that gears teaching styles to learning styles and that forges a stronger link between what students are asked to learn and what they will do with the rest of their lives.

A Look Back—Why a Change Is Needed

In the earlier part of this century, the industrial system in the United States was second to none in the world. Our industries flourished because of our economic strength, a proven approach to mass manufacturing, superior factories and equipment, and a workforce composed of strong managers and capable, compliant frontline workers. A college degree was considered a sure road to economic and professional success and the guarantee of a superior lifestyle that was improving each year. This concept became part of the American dream, and its perception has persisted into the present, even as the reality of the American job market has shifted.[1] For more than forty years, non-college-educated workers also felt assured of a comfortable, middle-class lifestyle if only they remained persistent and kept their noses clean. The message from our business community to most high school students was very clear: *If you don't plan to go to college, just finish high school*

I'm just dumb.

the easiest way you can. Then, when you receive your diploma, come to work at the plant or shop down the street. If you show up on time, keep your mouth shut, don't ask questions, and do what you're told, you can make a good living.

This system worked—until about 1980. That was when U.S. industries began facing the reality that they were competing in price and quality with companies from throughout the .world. Indirectly, our unskilled and semiskilled workers were competing with workers in third-world countries who could learn their jobs relatively quickly, achieve a comparable or superior level of quality, and remain satisfied with wages that were five to ten times lower than those of the American worker. The only way for American companies to remain competitive and within the United States was to make full use of information systems, sophisticated technology, and automation. This meant that fewer but higher-skilled workers would be needed. Delays in retooling and restaffing (or "upskilling") resulted in loss of market share and, consequently, loss of jobs.

At about the same time, a trend that had begun in the 1960s was drastically changing the face of American education. Over a period of several

---

1. Commission on the Skills of the American Workforce, *America's Choice: High Skills or Low Wages* (Rochester, NY: National Center on Education and the Economy, 1990).

decades, schools had been diverted from their traditional goal of educating and training students and were being asked to address (and solve) such emerging societal problems as drug abuse, decline of family values, disruption of communities, and disrespect for authority in any form. This trend and many others led to the decline of quality and achievement in public education for all but a few students.[2] By the early 1980s, reports were emerging on the crisis in American education, but very little was being done.

By 1984, American employers were calling for a new generation of workers to help them compete. Schools were being cited for the poor academic achievement of most of their students and for the inability of new workers to read, compute, and learn the skills and attitudes required for their jobs. A situation that had been allowed to develop over decades was expected to be remedied in a few years. It did not happen. Some progress was made in isolated areas, but the "report cards" on American schools did not improve significantly during the 1980s.[3]

And the problems are still with us today. The American education system is generally considered neither a place for a rewarding career nor the source of a top-notch education. In fact, U.S. schools are increasingly being rejected by students—as evidenced by the growing number of dropouts. And they are sources of growing disappointment for employers; mounting frustration for teachers, counselors, and administrators; and ongoing embarrassment on the part of national leaders who compare achievement of U.S. students in math, science, and technology to that of students in other countries. The result has been disinterested youth, undereducated adults, a workforce that has neutered U.S. businesses in global competition, a defection of good educators from the public schools, and an alarming trend in public policy toward turning the responsibility of education over to private enterprise, employers, and second-chance programs.

The losers in this national calamity are many—industry, commerce, teachers, communities, and families. But the biggest losers of all are the students, or at least the majority of the students—those high schoolers who are not on the road to a baccalaureate degree. These students are getting a second-rate education and are slipping into employment (or unemployment) in a second-rate workforce. If conditions don't change these students, who should form the mainstay of America's middle class, will be destined to lower-class wages and lifestyles. And if America loses its middle class, all Americans will suffer.

---

2. David P. Gardner et al., *A Nation at Risk: The Imperative for Educational Reform*, report of the National Commission on Excellence in Education (Washington, DC: Government Printing Office, 1983).

3. U.S. Department of Education, National Center for Education Statistics, "The Annual Gallup Poll of the Public's Attitude Toward the Public Schools," *Digest of Education Statistics 1992* (Washington, DC: Government Printing Office, 1993).

How can we alter this course for our students and our country? We must reform our schools so that all students can win—and this will require a system that recognizes and respects students with different interests, different abilities, and different learning styles. We must give more than lip service to the reality that a university education is not for everyone. And we must create in our high schools an alternative curriculum that compares in expected achievement and respectability with the college-bound plan, one that prepares all students for a productive and satisfying career.

I don't have a chance.

The good news is that the solution is already at hand!

For over a decade, educators and policymakers have studied the crises in our schools, examined our curricula, sought advice from researchers and employers, and tested new strategies, new teaching materials, new techniques, and new partnerships. From these efforts—and from good old American ingenuity and grit—has emerged a grass-roots educational reform for grass-roots America. Called Tech Prep/Associate Degree (TPAD) but widely known simply as "Tech Prep," this approach is far more than a warmed-over "vocational ed" or "articulation plan." Over the past two decades, TPAD has evolved into a powerful educational reform movement that has the potential to cure many of the ailments in public education and our future workforce.

Tech Prep/Associate Degree can be described very simply in terms of what it offers: a better education and career preparation than most young people and their predecessors have experienced in over thirty years. But, like so many simple definitions for very complex systems, this description does not tell why, who, when, or how. A more thorough definition can be found in a concept paper released in 1992 by the Organizational Affiliates of the National Tech Prep Network. This five-page position paper, the collective creation of representatives from twenty-two education, business, and scientific organizations, begins with this explanation:

> Tech prep is a sequence of study beginning in high school and continuing through at least two years of postsecondary occupational education. The program parallels the college prep course of study and presents an alternative to the "minimum-requirement diploma." It prepares students for high-skill technical occupations and allows either direct entry into the workplace after

high school graduation or continuation of study which leads to an associate degree in a two-year college.[4]

Tech Prep/Associate Degree is far more than a theoretical possibility; in fact, its components are already widely available. Successful Tech Prep models have been launched across the country and are available for examination. Public policies and funding have emerged, and over a thousand new TPAD consortia[5] have begun planning, designing, and implementing programs. A few of these consortia have caught the full vision of TPAD and are beginning to make the major systemic changes that will be required. But the ultimate success and endurance of this important national educational reform depend upon the ability of educators, employers, and community leaders to capture the Tech Prep vision and make it an institutional reality—nationwide.

An Educational "Wish List"—TPAD Fills the Bill

In September 1992, a diverse group of educators, employers and policy-makers[6] met together and formulated a set of six outcomes desired from the ideal (hypothetical) educational reform. These six elements, although not necessarily comprehensive, capture the collective vision of what most thoughtful Americans want in a system of public education, feel they are paying for, and deem essential to maintain the culture, lifestyles, leadership, and ideals they value in our society. And although this educational "wish list" was not formulated with Tech Prep/Associate Degree in mind, the goals and vision of TPAD provide these desired outcomes to a remarkable degree.

Outcome #1: Students are focused, interested, and achieving.

In the ideal scenario, all students would feel a sense of purpose for attending school. They would be able to make conscious choices for the course of study they pursue, which would clearly relate to what they would be doing after high school graduation. High achievement would be expected of all students. Course content would be presented in the context of how it may be used in life and work.

---

4. Organizational Affiliates of the National Tech Prep Network, *Tech Prep/Associate Degree Concept Paper* (Waco, TX: Center for Occupational Research and Development, 1992), 1–2 (see appendix for complete paper).

5. A Tech Prep/Associate Degree (TPAD) consortium is a formal relationship/stakeholder group consisting of at least one community college, public school system, employer, and community organization within the schools' service region.

6. United States representatives in the conference proceedings of Schools and Industry: Partners for a Quality Education, September 1992.

Outcome #2: Employers and labor organizations are satisfied with the abilities and advancement potential of new workers, and employers are willing to hire these workers.

Educational standards in an ideal school would be "outcome-based"; that is, achievement would be measured by demonstrable knowledge, skills, and abilities—not "seat time." Employers not only have a voice in setting the outcomes, they also provide a kind of quality check on the educational process by evidence of their interest in hiring the graduates.

Outcome #3: Workers are capable of learning new skills and progressing in careers.

Preparing students for careers is one important purpose of public education. But useful, effective occupational or technical education requires that the student not just be "trained" for entry-level job tasks, but also be given a solid foundation of academics—mathematics, language arts, science, reasoning, and problem-solving skills. In today's technically sophisticated society, it is both unfair and irrational to continue past practices of training some students in "head skills" and others in "hand skills"; good education is the appropriate blending of the two. Workers with a solid academic foundation will be able to learn new skills as they are needed, not only for maintaining their jobs in an ever-changing workplace, but for advancement toward higher career levels. An ideal educational scenario would provide this kind of foundation for all students, not just the university-bound.

Outcome #4: Parents feel that children are challenged and developed to their full potential for adulthood.

Reaching one's full potential requires, among other things, having a clearly defined interest or pursuit and being able to understand one's abilities and use them appropriately. Different young people exhibit different interests in types of education and types of careers. In an ideal school system they would be allowed to pursue their interests with dignity and constructive support. Roughly one-third of American young people will pursue and achieve baccalaureate or graduate degrees. The remaining two-thirds should not be condemned to a second-rate education or meaningless jobs. Parents and their children must recognize and respect alternate forms of education and job pursuits. (Employers certainly do!) Students who are not university-bound should have access to a well-thought-out educational plan that is respectable, that does not "close the door" to later university studies, and that holds high expectations for achievement in academics as well as "hands-on" vocational work.

Outcome #5: Businesses participate actively in the education/training process.

Employers hold a stake in the educational process because the quality (or lack of it) in their workforce depends on the quality of the education system. And employers must ultimately judge the quality of the educational system by their acceptance of its product. It would seem obvious, therefore, that employers should play an active role in the educational process. And yet in most technical education programs, the role of employers is usually limited to approving a faculty-designed curriculum and donating unwanted (often outdated) equipment. In an ideal educational reform, the employer's role would include not only participating fully in curriculum design and program evaluation, but also providing opportunities for student-employee mentoring and work-based learning experiences.

Outcome #6: Students/workers are fully informed and responsible for choosing and progressing in their career fields.

Most students are better motivated and achieve more in school if the curriculum relates clearly to their life experiences and career goals. But many students have limited or no knowledge about career options, opportunities, or the preparation necessary for a given career. An ideal educational system would introduce broad career awareness from the very earliest grades. It would work with employers in the community to introduce opportunities for exploration in interesting careers and would provide ample and appropriate information and guidance to help students make choices that are realistic in terms of their interests, abilities, educational resources, and employment opportunities. Career guidance would cover not only entry-level jobs, but also the requirements and rewards for advancement in a career ladder.

The Tech Prep/Associate Degree movement did not begin with the purpose of addressing all of these outcomes. But in less than a decade it has evolved in response to the educational/economic environment prevalent in our country. It has now grown in size and respect into the major reform movement in our schools and colleges. And we who have had the opportunity of watching it grow have become convinced that Tech Prep indeed carries the potential to provide the caliber of education this "wish list" implies and to provide it for *all* students, not just a few.

Where Does American Education Fall Short?

Quite clearly, most American education today doesn't even come close to living up to the ideal indicated by the educational wish list we have just reviewed. That's precisely why our education system needs a reform like Tech Prep/Associate Degree—because American schools are falling short in several critical areas.

Needed: Better Career Guidance and Opportunities

Most young people today move through high school and the years beyond with little clear idea about what they want to achieve vocationally. Many do not understand the basic concept of a career. They get their first jobs (often part-time or summer) because the jobs are easy to obtain or because friends are working in the same places. Their motivation is to "get some cash" to buy something they want or to gain more freedom in their lives—motivations that generally lead them to unskilled, low-paying, dead-end jobs in areas such as food service or retail sales. When they need or want more cash, they typically remain in the same kinds of jobs but increase their working hours (or work two jobs). As work time increases, school time decreases. Grades may fall, and dropping out begins to look desirable.

This all-too-common scenario takes place in part because schools do not systematically provide enough practical career information and guidance—or they fail to provide it early enough. The elementary years are not too early to begin exposing children to different groups of careers or career areas, introducing the concept of the career ladder, and explaining the educational requirements for entry and advancement in a career. The middle and high school years should feature opportunities for career exploration and curricula that connect what is learned in the classroom to what is needed at work.

Unfortunately, such systematic career guidance simply doesn't exist in many school systems. Most guidance activities—if they exist at all—focus on preparing students for professional levels of service or for abstract studies of the humanities. Students who are interested can learn what they must do to get into college or even, eventually, into medical school. But almost no one informs students that a biomedical technician with an associate degree will

*I've got other things
on my mind.*

begin employment at a 50 to 100 percent higher starting salary than an average B.A. graduate in history, sociology, or political science!

What happens as a result? Students leave secondary and postsecondary institutions (graduating or not) unprepared for anything but low-skill jobs and destined for a lifetime of low wages and frequent unemployment. Their only opportunity to break this pattern is to reenter the educational/training system through some form of second-chance program and to recover the opportunities that were lost the first time around because they really did not know (or believe) the facts. The fact is that well-paying jobs and rewarding careers are available in a variety of occupational fields for men and women who complete advanced skills training and have a sufficiently strong academic foundation to learn new skills and be retrained when the need arises.

It is interesting to note that many of the students enrolled in associate-degree occupational programs at community and technical colleges already hold bachelor's or master's degrees in a liberal arts or business field.[7] These students have a strong academic foundation and are finally well focused and interested in pursuing a career that goes somewhere. When they complete their associate degrees, they are well prepared for excellent job opportunities. But they are achieving this result after a huge waste of personal time and money and a significant drain on our country's educational resources—as compared to TPAD graduates, who realized similar opportunities six to ten years earlier!

Needed: A More Competitive Workforce

Many of America's most popular fast-food franchises hire from the "minimum wage" labor pool and design their work environment to accommodate the no-skills worker. Preparation and service are controlled by packaged, premeasured foods, preset cooking time and temperatures, premixed sauces, and premeasured soft drinks. Clerks operate cash registers that feature pictures of the products instead of numbered keys and computers that determine and distribute the return change from customer payments. Often the tasks that allow the most freedom and creativity are cleaning the tables, sweeping the parking lots, and scrubbing the bathrooms!

---

7. Mary Ann Roe, *Education and U.S. Competitiveness: The Community College Role* (Austin, TX: IC[2] Institute, 1989), 55.

This "manufacturing" approach to food preparation and sales is based on the same assumptions and techniques that U.S. manufacturers have employed during most of this century. The strategy is to put the money and responsibility into the design of repetitive assembly lines controlled by middle-level managers and quality checked by means of inspection and quotas. This allows—even mandates—a low-skilled, low-wage, compliant workforce.

The down side to this approach has always been worker dissatisfaction. Workers quickly become bored with the "assembly line" approach; they lose pride in their work because they do not see themselves as true participants in the enterprise, and as a result they care little for the quality of their work or for customer satisfaction. They have little opportunity for career progression and little incentive for retraining in new specialties, upgrading their abilities, or improving their interpersonal skills. And young people headed for such jobs quickly receive the message that what they learn (or do not learn) in school has little effect on their opportunities, wages, or advancement potential in their working career.

The only two facets of which these workers have been assured—until recently—were job security and adequate wages. Since the beginning of the last decade, however, American workers occupying the low-level jobs in manufacturing and services have found they were competing with workers throughout the world—and losing. The result has been a substantial lowering of income and, consequently, standard of living.[8]

Many U.S. businesses are now changing their approach to regain competitiveness through higher quality and higher productivity, using automated technology and drawing on the ideas, experience, and responsibility of *all* their workers. But to accomplish the transformation, these employers require substantially better mental and interpersonal skills from their frontline workers. This need poses a renewed challenge to our educational system.

In his recent book *Head to Head*, Lester Thurow, one of America's leading economists, sets the criteria for the future competition between the U.S., Europe, and Japan. He underlines our country's need for an organized educational system for the non-baccalaureate-bound:

> The problem with the U.S. is that there are too many people in college and not enough qualified workers. The U.S. has outstanding universities, but it is missing its middle. Too much training takes place on the job and therefore is

---

8. Commission on the Skills of the American Workforce, *America's Choice*, 1–7.

unsystematic. "Following Joe around," the American system of on-the-job training, simply isn't a system. The resulting skills are very narrow and do not lead to workers who can absorb new technologies.[9]

The miserable state of education for the non-baccalaureate-bound high school student is not the result of some subversive plot to destroy our middle class. Neither is it an unconscious act of neglect. Rather, it results from faulty assumptions on the part of employers, educators, and the public at large. A perceived need for an outmoded system of workforce deployment has teamed up with the erroneous belief that two-thirds of our students simply cannot learn foundational subjects like math and science and consequently can only be taught hand skills and worked like drones. The result has been devastating for students, educators, and employers alike.

We have signs that the design of the American workplace may be changing. We also now have clear evidence that non-baccalaureate-bound students *can* learn and use higher-level skills. The question is "Will we redesign our schools and prepare our teachers for this potential new paradigm in education?"

Needed: A More Effective Education for the Majority of Students

Public education in the U.S. has a commendable record of serving 45 percent of its students—the 30 percent who will attend and be successful in college and the 15 percent who are disadvantaged and/or have special needs. We are proud of our high achievers and have constructed all sorts of special programs and enhancements to reward and encourage high scores on college entrance exams. These efforts have been largely successful; many consider the U.S. higher-education system the finest of its kind in the world. At the same time, we have shown great compassion for the physically, emotionally, and mentally handicapped: the "slow students" with special needs who require special programs, special equipment, and lower student-to-teacher ratios. Overall, these two groups—the ones at the two ends of the educational achievement spectrum—have been served fairly well in our public schools.

But more than half of our students—those in the so-called "middle quartiles," the "average" students—are being served very poorly indeed. Data from the U.S. Department of Commerce indicate a large disparity in investment:

---

9. Lester Thurow, *Head to Head: The Coming Economic Battle Among Japan, Europe, and America* (New York: William Morrow, 1992), 275.

Relative to their respective sizes, for every dollar in taxpayer's money invested in the education of the non-college bound, fifty-five dollars is spent subsidizing those going on to college—a ratio that is neither fair nor efficient.[10]

And reports from a variety of sectors indicate that we're getting about what we pay for—very poor achievement. We get students like those profiled at the beginning of this chapter: bright (or able to learn), but underachieving, disinterested, and at risk for dropping out of school.

Student Group	Education's Score (How are we doing?)
High Achievers	**A–**
Average Students	**F**
Special-Needs Students	**B–**

A Scorecard for Public Education

Unfortunately, our response to poor achievement has in many cases been counterproductive. Instead of changing our *approach* to teaching these students, we have simply lowered our standards. If they fail a math or science course, we don't reconsider our methods; we give them a course we think they can pass—usually a watered-down one with less content or less rigorous requirements. Not surprisingly, these students tend to meet our low expectations. It is their scores that are causing U.S. students to be rated thirteenth and fourteenth out of fifteen in math and science when compared to students in foreign countries.[11]

The problems stemming from such lowered standards persist at the postsecondary level as well. Most of the students entering occupational studies at community and technical colleges have very poor academic backgrounds and limited proficiencies in math, science, and communications. (One community college in the northwest U.S. reported that 80 percent of all students applying to study electronics were severely deficient in

---

10. Thurow, *Head to Head*, 275.

11. International Association for the Evaluation of Educational Achievement, *Science Achievement in Seventeen Countries: A Preliminary Report* (New York: Pergamon Press, 1988), 60.

mathematics and required two courses before Algebra I.) Only a few of the occupational students entering most community colleges have had a course in laboratory science, and most of them cannot construct proper sentences, paragraphs, and reports.

Because of the low academic levels of entering students, approximately 35 percent of the typical postsecondary occupational/technical curriculum is remedial—course work that should have been learned before the students left high school. Technical courses are taught before the students have acquired a solid academic foundation, which means that the technical content cannot be mathematically or scientifically based. This approach prevents the students from acquiring the advanced skills they really need in the new workplace.

This vicious cycle of low achievement and low expectation is not necessary. It certainly does not mean that middle-quartile students are "dumb" or incapable of learning. Indeed, research and experience show that these students can succeed in higher-level courses if two factors exist:

- if we keep our expectations high, challenging students to do their best, and

- if we teach the content in the way the students learn best.

Unfortunately, those two "ifs" have yet to be a reality in the majority of American classrooms. As a result, two-thirds of our students remain educationally "needy," and our society as a whole suffers.

The Tech-Prep Strategy:
How Tech Prep Can Meet Our Country's Education Needs

Nearly all educators and public policymakers who focus on educational/economic issues agree on the need for educational reform and a stronger workforce, but a wide range of divergent views arise when we begin addressing specific strategies for accomplishing the reform. Given the needs outlined above, the Tech Prep/Associate Degree strategy offers the most comprehensive and most promising strategy for reshaping our educational system to benefit everyone involved.

The essence of today's TPAD strategy is a "4+2" articulated approach to secondary and postsecondary education. That is, the actual TPAD curriculum covers the four years of high school (grades nine through twelve) and the first two years of postsecondary education, although an effective TPAD program will require preparation prior to the ninth grade and should make provision for program completers to continue articulating to a baccalaureate degree (4+2+2) if they desire. As already indicated, TPAD is primarily directed toward middle-quartile students—those who do not plan to pursue a baccalaureate degree but who are not identified as having "special needs."

In addition to these "basics," TPAD strategy involves these three elements:

Tech Prep Is Education with a Career Focus.

TPAD programs (including "pre-TPAD" emphasis in early grades) are designed to provide students with sufficient career knowledge, awareness, and exploration so that by the ninth grade they can make (and are required to make) choices about the type of career they plan to pursue. Students are also required to choose how and where they will obtain the education and training necessary to prepare themselves for their career choice.

Who cares?

If they plan to enter a university after high school graduation, students commit to a carefully planned college-prep curriculum in high school. Likewise, if they choose TPAD, they commit to a different but equally well-planned curriculum leading to an associate degree in a particular occupational cluster (health, business, technology, agriculture, and so on). Both programs are designed to prepare graduates for employment in their chosen field. All students learn that working toward career goals in high school leads to future rewards: further educational opportunities as well as rewarding jobs with attainable career paths.

However, the career decisions that TPAD students make early in their high school experience do not lock them into—or out of—other opportunities. Instead, well-designed TPAD programs provide students with a wide range of options:

- They can change their career orientation by choosing a different cluster of future occupations.

- They can move into a college-prep program.

- They can elect to go to work immediately upon high school graduation and continue their studies toward an associate degree either part time or at a later date. (For financial and other reasons, it is likely that half of the TPAD high school completers will go to work immediately after high school graduation.)

TPAD's career focus also means that career relevance is built into the course work. Students are motivated because they realize that accomplishments in learning not only build pride and self-esteem, but also measure competency for anticipated fields of work.[12] In other words, "What you learn in school you can use on the job."

How is this career relevance accomplished? Through laboratories and real (or simulated) work environments where students can see theories, phenomena, processes, skills, and techniques applied in practical contexts. Students are taught the way they learn best—through hands-on activities, case studies, job profiles, group problem solving (focusing on real work problems), and on-the-job apprentice opportunities. They use real workplace equipment, perform actual job tasks, and develop valuable career proficiencies. In short, Tech Prep focuses on relating schoolwork to actual application in the workplace.

Tech Prep Is Technical Education with a Strong Academic Foundation— Taught the Way Most Students Learn.

Tech Prep/Associate Degree offers an alternate path of study to the college-prep approach, but it is not and should not be an "easy way" to get out of high school by taking watered-down courses in science, mathematics, and English. The advanced skills needed for employment in today's and tomorrow's workforce require workers who know *why* as well as *how* in their jobs. Skills training by itself—which many vocational and adult education programs provided in the past—is neither sufficient nor desirable in the new workplace.

Tech Prep is based on the premise that good technical education can be provided and attained if students have a solid academic foundation—a thorough understanding of basic math, science, and communications skills. In order to make that kind of foundation available to more students, Tech Prep calls for significant, systemic reform in public education. This reform, in essence, focuses more on *how* we teach more than on *what* we teach. It takes into consideration the learning styles of the majority of students and therefore adopts a more hands-on approach commonly known as "applied academics" or "contextual learning."

Experience over the past decade in the development and use of courses based on this approach shows that most students learn more content in these courses than do students (usually identified as high achievers) in the traditional abstract academics courses. Tech Prep programs based on contextual learning are already realizing high achievement in middle-quartile students. (More information about this is included in chapters 3 and 4.)

---

12. David A. Kolb, *Experiential Learning: Experience as the Source of Learning and Development* (New Jersey: Prentice-Hall, 1984).

Tech Prep curriculum design is based on the theme: "Build a foundation; build on the foundation." TPAD, in other words, requires the integration of academic and technical education at all grade levels (nine through fourteen). A well-designed TPAD curriculum provides students with a solid academic foundation early in their high school years—in the ninth and tenth grades. Subsequent technical education/training, both at the high school level and at the postsecondary level, can therefore focus on the more advanced skills (such as problem solving) that employers say they need. Instead of just learning the vocabulary, tools, and techniques of a particular job, students can acquire the background and abilities they need to understand what they are doing and to learn new skills as they advance up a career ladder.

Tech Prep Places Emphasis on Education/Training Opportunities Beyond High School.

Studies in recent years indicate at least two reasons why high school education (even under the Tech Prep assumptions of higher academic achievement and advanced skills) is not sufficient to prepare employees for the new workforce:

- Most new jobs will require formal education beyond high school but will not require a baccalaureate degree.

- Most new job applicants (high school and higher-education grad-uates) have little or no related work experience and require a significant component of school-to-work transition.[13]

For these reasons—and because of the type of outcome-based education that is fundamental to Tech Prep/Associate Degree—Tech Prep programs require close relationships and carefully designed articulation between secondary schools, technical and community colleges, and worksite learning environments provided by employers. These three aspects of the Tech Prep curriculum will be explored in detail in chapters 6 through 8.

Tech Prep: An Evolving Vision

Tech Prep/Associate Degree did not spring full-blown as a comprehen-sive approach to educational reform. It began with the design and testing of a few experimental articulated programs during the late 1970s and evolved gradually over a period of fifteen years or so. During that time it has been tested, challenged, adapted—and developed into its present mature form.

---

13. Roe, *Education and U.S. Competitiveness*, 55.

Tech Prep, or at least the "2+2 Tech Prep" concept that was originally envisioned (two years of high school plus two years of postsecondary education), began in the early 1980s in a series of workshops that combined the thinking of people working in vocational education, community colleges, and curriculum development.

At about the same time, Leno Pedrotti and I had become involved in designing model curricula for associate-degree technician programs in new and emerging technologies.[14] Two central characteristics of these new curricula were a strong math/science foundation and a move toward a "common core"—a basic set of materials that make up 70 percent of the course work for ten or twelve different technical majors (specialties). But community and technical colleges who implemented this new curriculum structure in more than a dozen states were faced with the dilemma of trying to teach an "advanced skills" program to their entering students, the majority of whom had little exposure to and very poor mastery of basic mathematics, science, and language arts.

Further research indicated that these students typically were products of the so-called "general track" high school curriculum. They were usually middle-quartile high school students who had a record of poor achievement in abstract academic subjects. Typically, these general-track students saw their high-school curriculum as pointless, nonchallenging, and usually boring. Many dropped out, and those who graduated were ill prepared for anything but low-skill, low-wage jobs. A significant number eventually showed

I just want to be on my own.

up at two-year postsecondary community and technical colleges because they needed more education and training. And many of these came in desperation after losing their jobs due to plant closings or layoffs caused by "upskilling" or reduction of the workforce.

Since the mid-1970s, community colleges have responded appropriately to the needs of these "neglected majority" students by lowering the standards and achievement levels of their associate-degree programs and providing many levels of remediation studies. Even then, fewer than 25 percent of these students obtained their associate degrees. Most of them continued to "shop at the educational buffet" and left after taking a few courses and finding some opportunity for employment.

---

14. Dan Hull and Leno Pedrotti, "Challenges and Changes in Engineering Technology," *Engineering Education,* journal of the American Society for Engineering Education (May 1986), 726–732.

During the time that Pedrotti and I had begun observing these problems, Gene Bottoms of the American Vocational Association and Dale Parnell of the American Association of Community and Junior Colleges had been researching them as well. In 1984, Bottoms, Parnell, Pedrotti, and I met to plan a national strategy to foster 2+2 articulation programs in technical education. By the next year, 1985, the publication of Parnell's landmark book *The Neglected Majority*, brought the deficiencies of the general-track high school education to national attention.

Parnell's book focuses primarily on the need to provide general-track high school students with a better education.[15] Parnell believes that these non-college-bound students need an occupationally related curriculum to inject purpose and meaning into their high school studies and to give them a reason for remaining in school. It was he who introduced the concept of Tech Prep as a high school alternative to college prep and proposed the term *Tech Prep/Associate Degree* for an educational program in which middle-quartile high school students prepare for community and technical colleges through well-defined, occupationally related, articulated curricula.

Tech Prep as originally conceived by Parnell, Bottoms, Pedrotti and me was designed as a 2+2 (secondary/postsecondary) program for general-track high school students, those who had no plans and little opportunity for a baccalaureate degree. Intended to connect the curriculum in the last two years of high school to community college occupational offerings leading to the associate degree, 2+2 Tech Prep called for a stronger foundation through applied-academics courses and for eliminating duplication of courses at the high school and postsecondary levels. It also provided, through a structured curriculum opportunity, for high school students to earn postsecondary credit for certain courses. And it aimed at giving opportunity, direction, and meaning to middle-quartile high school students by focusing them on career objectives and a curriculum that would lead to further education/training after high school.

In the period from 1985 until 1990, a number of Tech Prep pioneers emerged to put these sketchy Tech Prep ideals and guidelines into practice. Applied-academics curriculum materials were developed, tested, and disseminated, and dozens of secondary/postsecondary consortia formed and developed 2+2 articulated programs.

As a result of these efforts, success stories started to emerge from the Carolinas, Rhode Island, and Virginia to Oklahoma and Texas, Florida, California, and Oregon—reports of renewed student interest, achievement, and retention. Enough enthusiasm, documented success, and political per-suasion were generated to make Tech Prep the new focal point of the 1990 Congressional reauthorization of the Carl D. Perkins Vocational and Applied

---

15. Dale Parnell, *The Neglected Majority* (Washington, DC: Community College Press, 1985).

Technology Education Act. This piece of legislation received subsequent annual appropriations for Tech Prep, increasing from sixty million to over one hundred million dollars. By the early 1990s it had launched more than one thousand new Tech Prep consortia.

Today, even as it is sweeping the nation (an estimated five hundred thousand students enrolled in 1992–93), Tech Prep continues to evolve. It is rapidly becoming the major educational reform that our nation so desperately needs. And a significant factor in this evolution has been the marriage between Tech Prep and applied academics.

Someday I'll be a star.

Coincidental to the emergence of Tech Prep in 1984–85, a national effort had begun to provide academic curricula and materials that would teach experiential, hands-on learners more effectively. A consortium[16] was formed by the Agency for Instructional Technology (AIT), the Center for Occupational Research and Development (CORD), and the State Directors of Vocational/Technical Education for the purpose of developing curriculum materials in a secondary-level applied physics course called Principles of Technology. (Initially the consortium consisted of twenty-five states and two Canadian provinces. It has grown to include forty-nine states, two Canadian provinces, and Puerto Rico.)

Preliminary formative testing of student achievement indicated that middle-quartile students (most of whom are not abstract learners) could learn rigorous, mathematically based physics if the content were presented in the context of how it was used in life and work, if appropriate mathematics material was reinforced when it was needed, and if students were allowed to experience and quantify the physics in hands-on laboratories using equipment familiar to life and work experiences.

In 1986, when these results were realized, the State Directors of Vocational/Technical Education determined that this type of applied science was vital to reform in vocational and technical education and that similar curricula in biology, chemistry, mathematics, and language arts should be developed and made available to middle-quartile high school students who had an interest in an occupational type of education.

Over the period from 1984 to 1993, national consortia developed, tested, and successfully implemented applied-academics curriculum materials in

---

16. The term *consortium* as it is used here is defined differently than the *Tech Prep consortium*. The usage of *consortium* in this context refers to a stakeholder group of state education agencies and research organizations organized for the development of applied curricula.

the areas of physics, mathematics, biology/chemistry, and communications. The implementation and preliminary evaluation of these materials were greatly assisted by a fifteen-state initiative of the Southern Regional Educational Board (SREB) on "Using Applied Academics to Improve General and Vocational Education in the High Schools."[17]

Tech Prep and the applied-academics movements emerged nationally during the same period and had at least two common goals:

- providing a stronger academic preparation for middle-quartile high school students (who are mostly experiential learners).

- facilitating interest and a sense of purpose in education by infusing vocational and technical applications into teaching strategies for academically focused courses.

It was logical and natural, therefore, that these two movements would merge. The merger was identified and reinforced throughout the country in eleven Tech Prep workshops (from 1990–92) sponsored by CORD, the American Association of Community and Junior Colleges, and the National Association of State Directors of Vocational Technical Education Consortium. It was also recognized by *Tech Prep/Associate Degree: A Win/Win Experience,* a "how to do it" book that Dale Parnell and I wrote and by a section of the Carl D. Perkins Vocational and Applied Technology Education Act Amendments of 1990.[18]

Since the merger of Tech Prep and applied academics, the TPAD concept has continued to evolve and mature. In the past few years, several general trends have combined to make it the focal point of national educational reform:

- Many states have already eliminated the general track in secondary education because it has no focus or academic standards.

- Many math and science educators are recognizing that the "applied" or "contextual" approach is a more effective teaching strategy for middle-quartile high school students.

- Applied-academics courses are being concentrated at the beginning of a Tech Prep curriculum so that an appropriate math/science foundation can be laid for the teaching of advanced stills in later technical courses. (However, Tech Prep works best if technical and

17. Gene Bottoms and Alice Presson, *Improving General and Vocational Education in the High Schools* (Atlanta: Southern Regional Education Board, 1989), 2–5.

18. Carl D. Perkins Vocational and Applied Technology Education Act Amendments of 1990, Title III, Part E: "Tech Prep Education."

academic content continue to be integrated throughout the Tech Prep curriculum.)

- A "4+2" curriculum structure has emerged for Tech Prep/Associate Degree programs—a major shift from the simple 2+2 articulation that was originally envisioned. A 4+2 curriculum requires that the applied-academics courses begin in the ninth and tenth grades. Tech Prep has even begun to stretch beyond the "4+2" focus to affect the whole of elementary/secondary education, and clear paths are emerging for TPAD graduates to continue their education beyond the associate degree (4+2+2).

- More people are understanding that, because of its emphasis on a strong academic foundation and the breadth of its high school technical clusters, Tech Prep is not a system for tracking students out of opportunities in higher education. To the contrary, by improving academic competencies, it *opens* opportunities for many students— and it keeps their options open longer.

At least two other national initiatives are underway that should provide a positive impact on the TPAD reform movement. One entails efforts sponsored by U.S. Departments of Labor and Education to identify national employment standards for a variety of industrial and business groups. These "standards" can potentially serve as a collective voice of employers stating what they expect from the educational programs that prepare their workers.

A second initiative involves a number of pilot Youth Apprenticeship programs being developed by Jobs for the Future, the Council of Chief State School Officers, and others. These programs have resulted from careful study of the European apprenticeship systems and involve adaptations of those successful elements that appear to fit into the culture and goals of America's business, labor, and education. Early reports seem to indicate they can provide realistic and effective high school learning experiences. The common goals of TPAD and Youth Apprenticeship, together with the strengths that each can offer to the other, suggest a likely marriage that could serve only to accelerate the development of and improve the quality of both efforts.

The Tech Prep Vision: Making Educational Reform a Reality

Because it is meeting our nation's expectations and needs, Tech Prep/Associate Degree continues to develop into a total educational reform. As its enrollment grows and its influence broadens, it is rapidly gaining recognition as far more than an improved form of vocational education or a simple secondary/postsecondary articulation of course work. TPAD is truly a new approach to education that supplies a proven benefit to students, employers, and society as a whole—the benefit of open minds and open doors.

Not all of the thousand-plus existing TPAD consortia have caught the full vision of the mature TPAD. At this point, some have only developed articulation agreements on existing courses. Others are providing applied academics, but have not restructured the curriculum to teach advanced skills. Still, a growing number are viewing TPAD as a total reform and are making the tough, systemic changes necessary to reach its full, transforming potential.

What are these changes? I would propose at least eight:

1. We must recognize and respect an alternative path for high school students. Tech Prep is distinctive from the traditional college-prep approach—not in terms of lower standards, but in providing an alternate way for students to reach the same standards, and for a different purpose.

2. Teachers, parents, and administrators, must expect high achievement from average students. (Chapters 3 and 4 will show that this is a realistic expectation if we systematically adopt contextual approaches to teaching and learning and if we prepare teachers adequately for these changes.)

3. We must provide earlier, broader, more effective career-awareness and career-exploration opportunities in elementary and middle schools.

4. The TPAD curriculum must embody true integration of academic and technical education not only in applied-academics courses, but throughout the curriculum. (See chapters 4 and 5.)

5. We must expect and achieve better results—the teaching of advanced skills—from vocational and technical education at both the secondary and postsecondary levels. (See chapters 5, 6, and 7.) It's time for the United States to meet—and surpass—the standards of other industrial countries by providing an organized postsecondary education for those who are not university-bound.[19]

6. We must develop a truly seamless articulated secondary/postsecondary articulated curriculum, preferably one organized around occupational clusters—groups of related occupations requiring a similar background. (See chapters 5, 6, and 7.)

---

19. Thurow, *Head to Head,* 275.

7. The employers of America's new workforce must be equal partners with schools in the process of preparing new workers. This will require the fostering of mutual understanding and joint goals, the development of positive industrial/labor leadership in public education, and the creation of a curriculum and delivery system where employers can participate—not just observe. (See chapter 8.)

8. High school curricula must become more outcome-based, preparing students to demonstrate skills and competencies that meet the employment standards of various occupational categories.

The Tech Prep/Associate Degree approach to educational reform really can work—if we let it. Students like Sonya, Dwight, Jessica, Julio, Sam, and Becca *can* learn and excel. In fact, they can become the backbone of tomorrow's highly skilled, highly productive workforce—if we take the initiative to make some systemic changes at all local levels. It's time we opened our minds and changed our priorities in education so that we can open the door to recovering the majority of our nation's human assets.

We know how to do it.

The question is: Will we do what is necessary to create school systems where everyone has a chance to be a winner?

In the first chapter I am attempting to introduce a model or a vision for Tech Prep—to give a broad picture of why it is needed, for whom it is intended, and what it will do for students, schools, industry, and our country as a whole. I am also trying to show a little about how Tech Prep has grown from its vocational education roots to encompass a much broader educational spectrum. Even those of us who have been committed to this approach from the beginning have been impressed by its effectiveness, its flexibility, and its potential for transforming both the American educational system and the American workforce.

It's possible, however, that this very broad overview raises as many questions as it answers. Tech Prep/Associate Degree is only one of many approaches to educational reform, and the boundaries between these approaches are not always clear. In addition, Tech Prep's historical connection with vocational education and its particular vocabulary—*non-college-bound; applied academics*, even *technical*—may lead to misconceptions.

In the past four to five years I have taken part in literally hundreds of meetings, workshops, evaluations, and discussions about Tech Prep with educators, policymakers, and parents, and I have found that the same basic group of questions or issues or misconceptions about Tech Prep seems to emerge consistently. These questions are answered in some depth in later chapters, but in the following pages I would like to address them directly and specifically.

Many of the answers to these questions have come from the trial-and-error experi-

2.

"YES,

**Answering
Your Questions
about Tech Prep**

BUT..."

ences of the pioneering Tech Prep consortia around the country. And many of these answers are still in process. Tech Prep/Associate Degree is truly an evolving philosophy; what was once a small idea has grown into an approach to education with potential to make a significant impact on millions of students. Even though not all the data are in yet, Tech Prep is far from a theoretical, untried concept. Tech Prep is here, and Tech Prep works. Here's how it's done.

Question #1: How is Tech Prep really different from vocational education? Couldn't we just modify vocational education to attract more students?

Tech Prep owes a great debt to vocational education for its origins and for much of its early support. Developing a more efficient and applicable vocational curriculum was part of the early and original intention for Tech Prep and especially for 2+2 programs. But as the national economy and the employment picture have changed, the vision for Tech Prep has had to change as well. Even with "improvements," the model of vocational education that served us so well in the 1950s and 1960s and even in the 1970s is just not capable of preparing students for the world where they will live and work or of providing employers with the kinds of workers they need to stay competitive. And traditional vocational education programs cannot even come close to reaching all the students who could benefit from Tech Prep.

Tech Prep not only trains people to get their first job, it also prepares them for an entire career, and it prepares them for further education and training—that is, they "learn to learn." The Tech Prep/Associate Degree curriculum clearly cannot be a "patch-up job" on existing vocational or technical programs. Because TPAD provides the students an early, solid academic foundation, the entire curriculum structure must change to build on this strong academic foundation.

The traditional "voc-ed" model was geared primarily to kids who were considered "not college material." It was based on the assumption that these students not only had poor academic aptitudes (couldn't learn "real" math, science, and English) but also would have little need for such "head skills" on the job. As a result, voc-ed concentrated primarily on teaching hand skills geared to specific tasks. Students were usually taught "how" with very little attention to "why." And although periodic attempts were made to infuse academics into the vocational education program without changing the overall structure or philosophy of the program, these curriculum changes gave little evidence of improving the academic competency of vocational students.

Meanwhile, the job market in the United States was changing dramatically. Discussions with employers in business and industry about the kinds of skills that were needed for the new workers and reviews of the general and vocational curriculum revealed important reasons that just modifying vocational education was not enough. Employers said that *all* workers needed a much better academic foundation and that they needed to know *how to use* these academic skills in the workplace. Job-specific skills were not enough and were quickly outdated. But academic skills that just prepared students to learn more academics were not sufficient either. Workers needed to be taught to *transfer* what they learned in class into the work environment.

From this awareness grew the need for the *integration* of academic and technical education—infusing the technical applications into the academic courses. (Look for this discussion in more depth in chapter 5.) And from the awareness that most vocational and general education students had not performed well in traditional academic subjects grew the need for a different approach to teaching—an *applied* or *contextual* approach (see in depth explanations in chapters 3 and 4). These two concepts—integration of academics with applications and contextual learning—along with the idea of *competency-based* education, are at the heart of what makes Tech Prep so distinctive and so promising.

Question #2: Why should we invest our money, time, and efforts into a "reform" that focuses on only the "technical" careers?

I think the response to this question really has a lot to do with how you define *technician*—and that term as used in Tech Prep/Associate Degree covers much more ground than many people think.

Because of my engineering background I have always tended to think of technicians as the people who work along with engineers in such fields as energy generation, manufacturing, telecommunications, microcomputer technology, and electronics. And Tech Prep/Associate Degree has been very successful in preparing students for these kinds of careers.

However, the Tech Prep/Associate Degree curriculum, instruction, and guidance methods have proved so sound and flexible that they have adapted to many career areas not commonly thought of as "technical"—primarily those that require skills beyond a high-school diploma but not necessarily a baccalaureate degree. Thus, for the purposes of Tech Prep/Associate Degree, *technician* has come to include professionals and paraprofessionals such as nurses, bookkeepers, paralegals, dietitians, elder-care workers, law-enforcement officers, plant operators, physical therapists, and fashion designers—and many more.

Through the input of the business community, *local* Tech Prep consortia have the option to implement specific career programs that will have the greatest impact on local economic development and will provide the greatest opportunities for students in terms of seeking employment after they have finished their education. This is why it is so critical that Tech Prep continue to be a local educational reform initiative.

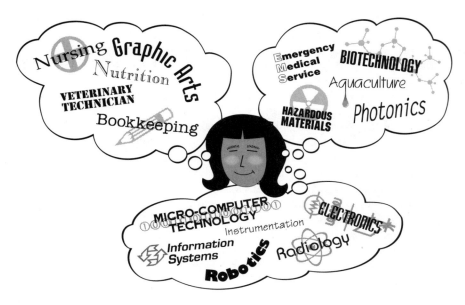

Figure 1. A Technical Career for Me?

Question #3: Aren't we gearing a school to the lowest common denominator if we enroll our general education students in Tech Prep? It seems we are encouraging a lesser alternative to college prep for the "dumb kids."

In our culture, the definition of success in education continues to be the achievement of a "college education," and most people assume that means a bachelor's or even a graduate degree. But the simple fact is that not all high school students will—or necessarily should—attend a university or receive a baccalaureate degree.

For a number of reasons ranging from lack of money to lack of confidence to lack of interest, fewer than one-third of the American young people in today's high schools will finish a four-year college degree (about all we need in our workforce). But this does *not* mean that two-thirds of our kids are fated to settle for second-rate jobs and second-rate opportunities. In fact, Tech Prep is specifically designed to *raise* the common denominator in our schools and keep the doors of opportunity open for much larger numbers of students.

The current and future workplace does demand more advanced levels of skill and knowledge than high schools normally provide, but fewer than one-third of the occupations in this country actually require the kind of education and preparation that a university degree provides. The majority of occupations in today's marketplace (about 60 percent) call for some postsecondary education and training, but not necessarily a baccalaureate degree. And many of these occupations pay very well; many associate-degree graduates just out of school are generating salaries higher than most bachelor of arts graduates.

Tech Prep/Associate Degree opens doors for students because it does not allow them to graduate from high school without a plan for their future and a solid education that prepares them for postsecondary schools and for the workplace. Tech Prep/Associate Degree is not a lesser alternative or a track to nowhere, but an option that builds several pathways (not tracks!) for future careers and educational opportunities.

In a typical Tech Prep/Associate Degree program, for instance, about 25 to 30 percent of Tech Prep students will go directly to work after high school graduation. These students will have not only the skills they need to get a decent entry-level job, but also a sufficient academic background to continue their education later if they choose.

Another group of Tech Prep students—more than half of those who begin a Tech Prep program—will complete the entire course of study and obtain their associate degree and perhaps certification in their particular specialty. They will then go to work in the field of their choice.

Still another 10 percent of Tech Prep students will follow a third path and go on to pursue a baccalaureate degree. They may do this either by switching to a college-prep curriculum in high school or by first obtaining their associate degree and then going on to the university. Although relatively few Tech Prep students will end up pursuing this option, the stronger academic foundation they have built in their Tech Prep courses will make the option possible, if they choose it, with little or no remediation. In fact, some students may choose to go on to the university because Tech Prep has given them a new self-confidence and an interest in the field they are pursuing.

Far from "tracking" students or limiting their options, Tech Prep/Associate Degree keeps doors open for students. In chapters to come, I explain how the curriculum design and teaching methodology of Tech Prep ensure this flexibility and strength.

Question #4: How can we expect average students to complete higher levels of academics, when they are failing in the lower-level courses now? Doesn't this set students up for failure and dropping out?

There are two ways to make sure that students meet a certain set of expectations: One is to make the curriculum easy enough for anyone to pass, and the other is to change the way in which the curriculum is taught.

Unfortunately, the first strategy has been the more common response to poor achievement in recent years. In many cases, instead of changing our approach to teaching students, we have simply lowered our standards. If they failed a course, we didn't reconsider our methods; instead we gave them a course we thought they could pass. This usually meant watered-down content or less rigorous requirements.

Tech Prep is built on the second response. Instead of assuming that the poor-achieving students failed, it assumes that the system failed them. Rather than making course work easier, it aims at teaching it differently, using methods and approaches that are more consistent with the way most students learn. In most cases this means more hands-on exploration and more real-world application.

In chapter 4, I discuss what cognitive scientists and learning theorists have discovered about how *contextual learning* can empower students to perceive and process knowledge, accept the value of the knowledge, and transfer that into life and work. Tech Prep/Associate Degree draws heavily on those discoveries, and the positive results of its *applied-academics* approach already can be seen in terms of higher achievement and lower dropout rates.

An important side benefit to this "teach as much, but teach differently" approach has been a marked increase in student confidence. Many students enrolled in Tech Prep have experienced success at school for the first time in their lives, and they have felt affirmed by educators, employers, parents, and other members of the community because they are involved in a respectable program that is not perceived as less than what should be expected of all students.

Question #5: Will a Tech Prep/Associate Degree student lose the opportunity to enroll in "liberal arts" courses such as history and social studies—or even electives like art, photography, and sports—that aren't specifically job-oriented?

The simple answer to this question is no. First of all, Tech Prep students, like all students, will be expected to meet their state's high-school graduation requirements, which include courses in history, humanities, and other essential curricula. And although certain career-specific electives are built into the Tech Prep curriculum, students will have access to some general electives as well. (Each Tech Prep consortium must deal with these issues on a local level according to the requirements within the state and local school systems.) Tech Prep/Associate Degree is not a way for students to "get out of" a solid basic education, but a way to keep students moving and motivated because they can see where their education is leading them.

Like any good curriculum plan, Tech Prep/Associate Degree curriculum is carefully planned to build from a broad course of study to a more particular specialization. The Tech Prep/Associate Degree program begins first with a basic core curriculum which includes required courses (e.g. mathematics, humanities, social sciences). Students then move into a technical core curriculum—courses that provide a foundation for a cluster of occupations (e.g. health-related careers). Finally, as students continue through their associate-degree program, they complete a specialty curriculum (courses specific to a career interest, e.g. nursing). Throughout the program, Tech Prep/Associate Degree students will still have the option to take elective courses, although they must complete required courses in their major (career cluster) in order to be recognized at the postsecondary school.

The specific academic requirements for a Tech Prep/Associate Degree course of study will depend upon the major (career cluster) that the student chooses as well as the local and state requirements. For instance, a Tech Prep student enrolling in the engineering technology cluster must fulfill more math and science requirements than a Tech Prep student enrolling in fashion merchandising. But no matter what major the Tech Prep student chooses, the core academic requirements should be *higher* than what would be required of a student on a traditional general high school track. Many of the courses required for the Tech Prep student are the same in content and number as the college-prep student. In chapter 5, I explain the design and structure of the Tech Prep/Associate Degree curriculum in more depth.

Question #6: Isn't Tech Prep just a fancy name for "tracking" students—forcing them to make binding decisions about their futures when they are really too young to make those kinds of decisions?

Tech Prep/Associate Degree does require students to begin making some decisions about their future by the end of their eighth-grade year. However, they are not being asked to lock themselves into an inflexible track that will determine the whole course of their lives. Essentially, they are being asked only:

- to think seriously about the kind of career they eventually would like to pursue and

- to choose a plan to follow instead of drifting through high school with no purpose.

In fact, the only major decision that eighth-grade completers are currently asked to make is to choose Tech Prep as opposed to college (baccalaureate) prep. That means that in the ninth and tenth grades these students will begin taking a foundational curriculum that includes some applied academics and career exploration in addition to the general courses required by the state for graduation.

And it is important to note that the Tech Prep/Associate Degree curriculum is flexible enough not to lock students into an unchangeable path—or out of other opportunities. As we have seen, the skills that Tech Prep students will have achieved upon high school graduation should be high enough to qualify them, without additional training, for entry-level jobs in their field of interest. If they choose to continue their program of study, their courses will automatically articulate (connect) to the community college and should launch them into an advanced-skills and/or advanced-placement program. Decisions to enter a university or to change a career focus are also available to the Tech Prep students because they have laid a solid academic foundation before moving into their specialty areas.

Some of these changes, like any shift in long-term goals, will require that the students go back and take some specialty courses that their new fields of study require. Most changes, however, will require a minimum of "backtracking."

Crucial to helping students make informed choices about their course of study in Tech Prep is a sufficient and broad career awareness. By at least the ninth or tenth grade, preferably earlier, students should have been exposed to a wide array of accurate information about possible careers and what they require. Tech Prep consortia are building the career-awareness element into their programs in the middle schools. A pre-Tech Prep emphasis in the elementary and middle schools gives students an even earlier opportunity to explore careers before choosing courses of study.

By ninth grade, most Tech Prep students will have chosen a broad career interest (health, business, engineering, and so on) and will be learning more about what the various specialties entail in their applied-academics courses and in the technical core courses (Anatomy Physiology, Introduction to Aerospace, Electronics, and so on). By the twelfth grade, Tech Prep students will have chosen a specific career specialty and will be much closer to achieving a career goal, although even then they will not be locked into an inflexible future.

There are many different ways in which the schools can support students and their parents in making decisions about their future careers and their course of study. Many Tech Prep/Associate Degree consortia involve middle-school counselors to guide students, while other consortia have hired individuals from the business community to offer full-time career counseling. Mentoring programs have also played a strong role in helping students decide what careers are best for them. School-to-work programs, co-ops, and youth apprenticeship programs are often the best way for students to learn about and assess their career interests at the same time (see chapter 8).

Question #7: Why should we implement Tech Prep instead of some other reform such as Youth Apprenticeship?

While I would like to say that Tech Prep/Associate Degree is the be-all-and-end-all of educational reform, that is simply not the case. Although Tech Prep is a viable solution to the educational problems of the forgotten half of students, it is not the only answer to our educational woes. But we don't have to have only one answer. One of the great strengths of Tech Prep from my viewpoint is its flexibility; it can peacefully coexist with a number of different but compatible initiatives, including Youth Apprenticeship.

For instance, the basic ideas set forth by the various Youth Apprenticeship initiatives that have been proposed for our country are really very similar to those of Tech Prep: integration of academic and vocational curricula, seamless articulation between high school and secondary schools, outcome-based educational standards, and strong partnerships with industry. Youth Apprenticeship even goes one healthy step farther than most Tech Prep programs in encouraging more worksite learning. While not all Tech Prep/Associate Degree consortia may find the definition or name of Youth Apprenticeship useful, I believe the basic ideas of worksite learning and cooperative learning are important for inclusion in any Tech Prep curriculum. I certainly don't believe we have to choose one and exclude the other.

Although I propose an ideal model for a Tech Prep/Associate Degree curriculum in chapter 5, the reality is that Tech Prep is beginning to represent the generic structure of any school-to-work transition curriculum, and there is plenty of room to include Youth Apprenticeship initiatives within the Tech Prep/Associate Degree structure. In fact, my conversations with Youth Apprenticeship leaders and implementers have convinced me that most favor the kind of curriculum structure that Tech Prep offers to the traditional general studies curriculum structure.

What we have done in Tech Prep over the last ten years is to build and evolve a very sound, tested curriculum structure with room for many options—and these options may well include other initiatives such as Youth Apprenticeship. Among the other independent school reform ideas and initiatives that are already being adopted in conjunction with some Tech Prep programs are course integration, competency-based curriculum, reading and writing across the curriculum, total quality management, and teaching to SCANS (Secretary's Commission on Achieving Necessary Skills).

This basic compatibility of Tech Prep with other initiatives may sometimes be obscured by defensiveness on the part of educational leaders who have developed their own programs and established their own goals for their schools. These educators may see Tech Prep as a competitive reform and be threatened by it.

The administrators of one school district, for instance, resisted the ideas behind Tech Prep because they saw it as competing with their own initiative.

However, when I had the opportunity to explain the fact that Tech Prep is basically a philosophy that can be adapted to the needs and concerns of a particular school system, they began to see that Tech Prep could work in partnership with their own plans for the district. Now they are enthusiastic proponents of Tech Prep/Associate Degree and effective leaders in making Tech Prep a success in their school and community.

Question #8: How do you really know that Tech Prep is going to work?

We already have measurable evidence that existing Tech Prep programs are successful; I cite some of that evidence later in this book. However, it is difficult to test a bridge before it is completely built, and it is equally difficult to measure fully the success of Tech Prep before programs have matured and more students have had an opportunity to progress through the programs.

It is important to remember that Tech Prep is a relatively new initiative and one that is still evolving. Even its earliest, most primitive forms are less than ten years old as I write this book, and full-fledged Tech Prep/Associate Degree programs are just now in the process of being fully implemented. Every day practitioners are discovering new approaches and new ideas.

How do you evaluate a program when it is still evolving? It's not easy, although some federal requirements for the evaluation of Tech Prep have stirred a lot of debate among educators and public servants. However, some of the elements of Tech Prep, such as applied academics and articulation, have been in place long enough to show some results, and these give an indication of the kind of success we can expect from Tech Prep.

For instance, as I show in chapter 4, we are beginning to amass some reliable data concerning the effectiveness of applied-academics courses, which provide the academic foundation of the Tech Prep curriculum. These early studies indicate that Tech Prep's applied-academics approach is indeed effective in teaching subjects such as math, physics, biology, and chemistry to middle-quartile learners.

In addition, as I indicate in chapter 6, some of the prototype Tech Prep programs are already beginning to show positive results in terms of a lowered dropout rate and an increase in the number of students enrolling in postsecondary institutions. Although no hard data have been compiled as yet, the experience of these pioneer programs is that getting more of these average and middle-quartile students engaged in education that makes sense to them—which means personal and occupational/career emphasis—reaps significant benefits.

The final test of an educational initiative of this type, of course, is whether the program produces graduates who can really perform in the workplace—whether employers are satisfied with employees who have come out of Tech Prep programs. Here again, because Tech Prep is relatively new, the number of students who have completed the program and entered the workforce is relatively small. But certain employers are already showing a preference for hiring Tech Prep graduates.

Is Tech Prep building a foundation for learning? Are we lowering the dropout rate and getting more students interested in school? Are more students pursuing higher education? Are employers satisfied with their new employees? While it's still too early for a definitive yes, I believe we do have compelling evidence that all of these things are happening—and will happen—as a result of the Tech Prep initiatives. I spell this evidence out more fully in chapters to come.

Question #9: Where will the money come from?

Federal funds are now available, in the form of Tech Prep grants, for launching Tech Prep initiatives: planning, training teachers, and doing whatever is necessary to get a Tech Prep program off the ground. This "seed" money is now being authorized in excess of a hundred million dollars a year to be doled out to different states.

Eventually, however, Tech Prep must be recognized as a significant component of public education. To continue to grow and improve, it must be seen as important enough to demand its fair share of local and state public-education money. In other words, when Tech Prep consortia get beyond the initial funds and implementation, the real issue becomes that of institutionalizing funds for Tech Prep.

For local school systems, this means that Tech Prep programs will eventually become part of the overall school budget. Some of this can be managed by redistributing funds; eliminating the general education track, for instance, may free up some money, or an overlap with vocational programs may provide some resources. However, money may also need to be taken from programs that support only the upper- or lower-quartile students.

Tech Prep is specifically earmarked to serve the majority of students in the public schools—students who typically have been underserved in our school systems. In the past, it has been hard to find a line item in federal, state, or local education budgets to support the middle majority of students. But these students deserve an educational program that appropriately supports their needs—that opens up their minds to learning and opens doors for them into the future. Tech Prep is that kind of program—and it's worth the money.

3.

LEARNING

**Cognitive Science
and Its Practical
Applications**

IN CONTEXT

Like many teachers, Linda Durham is frustrated. She knows her students need the mathematical concepts she teaches, but she finds it difficult to reach students who struggle with math or lack the motivation to learn what she teaches. To illustrate this point, she describes the learning behavior of three of her students, Karla, Tony, and Dave.

Karla is a responsive student, but she never quite seems to "get it." She listens to explanations, takes notes from the board, and completes her homework assignments. However, she struggles with word problems from the text and on tests. Karla reads at her age level and can usually manipulate equations when the directions are very clear, but she cannot seem to develop strategies to solve problems when they are presented in written text instead of numerical format. She is confused by the relationship between the words and the numbers.

Tony gets by in math by using his knack for memorizing the steps of a problem. He copies Linda's examples and even does well with stated problems as long as he has a pattern to follow. But when a problem is stated in a different context or a variable is changed, he fails to transfer previously learned skills to a new situation. Tony, not recognizing the limitations of his mechanistic approach, complains that problems modified outside of his pattern are "tricky."

Dave considers math a complete bore. During class, Linda finds him drawing pictures or sleeping. When she asks him to pay attention, Dave usually responds with "Why? I'll never need this stuff. I don't think that I should have to take this class." Linda notices, however, that when she involves

Dave with other students in the class he responds better to the concepts and shows improvement on his tests.

Linda recognizes that the learning behaviors of these three students are similar to the behaviors of many of the students she has taught in the past. Karla knows it is important to study math, but she has trouble understanding its meaning and relevance outside of the numerical context. Tony knows only that he can often rely on memorized tricks to solve for the right answer; the meaning and application of his work are irrelevant to him. Dave tunes out completely when Linda stands up at the blackboard. All three of these students struggle with connecting mathematical concepts to the physical world because they have a perception that this material has no particular value to their personal lives or future.

And Linda, like many teachers, is desperately seeking ways to reach and motivate these students—to help them understand not only the specific math concepts she is teaching, but also the value and usefulness of math in their lives. She suspects that each one could learn the material better if she could gear her teaching to the way the student learns. But she does not have time within the confines of the standard classroom structure to work with each of them separately.

The above scenario, which is based on conversations with several math teachers, illustrates some of the various ways students typically respond to the concepts taught in a classroom and the learning behavior most teachers encounter on a daily basis. If Tech Prep is about school reform, it must place priority on helping teachers like Linda facilitate improved teaching and learning for all their students. It must feature teaching methods that open minds for effective, useful learning.

Facing the Challenge

What *is* the best way to convey the many concepts that are taught in a particular class—or any other class—so that *all* students can use and retain that information? How can the individual lessons be understood as interconnected pieces that build upon each other? How can a teacher communicate effectively with students who wonder about the reason for, the meaning of, and the relevance of what they study? How can we open the minds of Karla, Tony, and Dave for learning concepts and techniques that will open doors of opportunity for them throughout their lives? These are the challenges teachers like Linda face every day, the challenges that a curriculum and an instructional approach based on *contextual learning* can help them face successfully.

The inability to make connections and to understand the value and meaning of the curriculum is not unique to these three students. The majority of students in our schools are like Karla, Tony, and Dave in that the way they process information and their motivations for learning are different from the traditional methods in the classrooms. They have a difficult time understanding academic concepts (such as math) as they are commonly taught, but they desperately need to understand these academics in relationship to the workplace and to the larger society in which they will live and work.

As the need for higher levels of academic and work skills increases, the challenge to assist all students in mastering these skills grows stronger. In many schools across the country over the last five years, I have seen Tech Prep become the agent for change in this area—opening doors for a fresh approach to the teaching/learning process.

Tech Prep/Associate Degree curricula require of the average student not only a stronger academic foundation and a higher caliber of work skills, but also a better understanding of how academic concepts relate to the workplace and how vocational skills connect with these academic concepts. This is a higher level of learning that is not usually taught to the above-average student, much less to the average student, who needs it most. Traditionally, students have been expected to make these sorts of connections on their own, outside of the classroom.

However, growing numbers of teachers today are discovering that most students' interest and achievement in math, science, and language improve dramatically when they are directly assisted in making connections between new information (knowledge) and experiences they have had or other knowledge they have already mastered. Students' involvement in their schoolwork increases significantly when they are taught *why* they are learning the concepts and *how* those concepts can be used outside the classroom. And most students learn much more efficiently when they are allowed to work cooperatively with other students in groups or teams and to learn from one another.

Many different terms have been used to describe this approach to teaching—*hands-on*, *real world*, *apprenticeship*, and *work-based*. In my curriculum work (and in this book), I have frequently used the term *applied academics* to refer to specific courses that incorporate these ideas in the curriculum. However, I have come to prefer the term *contextual learning* to describe the overall philosophy of learning that underlies Tech Prep reform.

The Contextual Approach to Learning

Contextual learning is an emerging concept that incorporates much of the most recent research from the cognitive science (the science of the mind). It also is a reaction to the essentially behaviorist theories that have dominated American education for many decades. The contextual approach recognizes that learning is a complex and multifaceted process that goes far beyond drill-oriented, stimulus/response methodologies.

According to contextual learning theory, learning occurs only when students (learners) process new information or knowledge in such a way that it makes sense to them in their frame of reference (their own inner world of memory, experience, and response). This approach to learning and teaching assumes that the mind naturally seeks meaning *in context*—that is, in the environment where the person is located—and that it does so through searching for relationships that make sense and appear useful.

Building upon this understanding, contextual learning theory focuses on the multiple aspects of any learning environment, whether that is a classroom, a laboratory, a worksite, or a wheat field. It encourages educators to choose and/or design learning environments that incorporate as many different forms of experience as possible—social, cultural, physical, and psychological—in working toward the desired learning outcomes.

In such an environment, students discover meaningful relationships between abstract ideas and practical applications in the context of the real world, and concepts are internalized through the process of discovering, reinforcing, and interrelating these relationships. For example, a physics class studying thermal conductivity might be allowed to measure how the quality and amount of building insulation material affect the amount of energy required to keep the building heated or cooled. Or a biology or chemistry class might learn basic scientific concepts by studying the spread of AIDS or the ways in which farmers suffer from and contribute to environmental degradation.

Curricula and instruction based on this approach will be structured to encourage many different forms of learning in context, such as:

- *Relating:* learning in the context of life experiences.

- *Transferring:* learning in the context of existing knowledge—using and building upon what a student already knows.

- *Applying:* learning in the context of how the knowledge/information can be used.

- *Experiencing:* learning in the context of exploration, discovery, and invention.

- *Cooperating:* learning in the context of sharing, responding, and communicating with other learners.

Such curricula have the potential to create an environment in which all students, including Karla, Tony, and Dave, are more empowered in their learning experiences. The different contexts in which they learn will broaden their abilities to make connections, enjoy discovery, and use knowledge—abilities that they will practice throughout their life and career.

A Systemic Approach to Educational Reform

Total Quality Management, an approach to business that is effectively practiced by many organizations, is based on the concept of *systemic change*. Proponents of this theory assert that 92 percent of business errors can be attributed not to incompetent individuals, but to problems in the overall system of operation. The best way to improve efficiency, therefore, is to change the system.

Successful efforts to incorporate contextual learning into the classroom are based on a similar assumption—that to effect positive changes in the way our students learn, we first must reexamine and change the way the educational system works. This in turn will lead to changes in curriculum and instruction techniques. And when this happens, student attitudes, behavior, self-confidence, and interest will inevitably increase.

In what ways must our current American system of education change? Economist Anthony Patrick Carnevale points to a number of elements he believes have caused many American students to lose (or never to attain) the knowledge they need outside the classroom—all problems that can be satisfactorily addressed by a curriculum based on contextual learning. His report, *America and the New Economy*, prepared for the United States Department of Labor, asserts that

> American schooling sequesters students from the real world [and thus tends to inhibit learning because it]
> - breaks knowledge down artificially into theoretical disciplines,
> - breaks disciplines down into component pieces, and
> - demands that students commit fragments of knowledge to memory.
> - Applications are reserved for pen-and-paper exercises at the back of the chapter.
> - Interdisciplinary applications are rare, and applications in the context of working groups are even more rare.[1]

Throughout our century the American educational system has continued to break down and divide disciplines and concepts to make education less concrete and more theoretical. The assumption was that by breaking down the body of material into separate subjects and endeavors students could focus on the learning task itself. This way, theories that had been learned first could be applied to specific situations encountered at a later time.

---

1. Anthony Patrick Carnevale, *America and the New Economy*, report prepared for the United States Department of Labor (Washington, DC: Government Printing Office, 1991), 14.

In recent years, however, that system has only predisposed students to take a more or less passive and mechanistic approach to learning. (Because they have no real understanding of how knowledge can be applied in their lives, they can only try to take in what has been dished out with no sense of actually using it.) In addition, the limited focus for learning has resulted in more rigid structures and rules within the schools ("Sit still!" "Be quiet.") and fewer opportunities for exploration, discovery, and application.

Interestingly, the traditional educational practices described by Carnevale mirror the mass-production model followed by American industry in the earlier part of this century. Manufacturing processes were broken down into small mechanical tasks, and individuals were asked to carry out those tasks with little regard to or understanding of the complete product.

As technology has reformed the workplace, however, this fragmented approach is proving less and less effective. Today's employees must have a better basic understanding of how entire systems work. It's not enough to be a cog in the wheel; employees need to understand how and why the wheel works.

And educators as well as employers are experiencing a need to transform their work and teaching environments—to teach individuals to make connections between theory and practice, between one discipline and another, between head skills and hand skills. Education must undertake the task of integrating what traditionally has been fragmented to strengthen the students' understanding of whole systems, to accommodate the different ways that they learn, and thus to prepare them more effectively both for the workplace and for future learning. This process of integration lies at the heart of contextual learning.

Correcting False Assumptions About Learning

But contextual learning offers more than a tool for defragmenting the American educational system. It also provides a more effective approach to teaching the majority of students because it is specifically geared to the way these students learn.

In recent years, cognitive science and studies of the relationships between structured learning and the work environment have given us a better basis to evaluate the effectiveness of various methods of teaching and learning. Many educators, however, tend to interpret the learning environment according to their own experience as students. In other words, they teach the way they have been taught—usually through traditional, abstract, lecture methods.

But while the traditional classroom model is a valid one, it is not necessarily the most effective strategy for teaching the majority of students. To increase their effectiveness in the classroom, many educators may need to change some of their basic assumptions about how people learn.

Dr. Sue Berryman of the Institute on Education and the Economy at Columbia University has isolated five common misconceptions about the ways people learn—assumptions that may well be blocking many students from an effective learning experience. In each case, the contextual learning approach can help correct the false assumption and the inefficient educational processes that grow out of the assumptions.[2]

False Assumption #1: People predictably transfer learning from one situation to another.

Berryman questions, for example, whether most people actually use in everyday practice the knowledge, skills, and strategies they acquired during their formal education. For instance, a student training to be a radiology technician may have difficulty relating the theories she learned in physics class to the technical skills she is learning in her electronics courses.

---

2. Sue E. Berryman and Thomas Bailey. *The Double Helix of Education and the Economy* (New York: Institute on Education and the Economy, Columbia University, 1992), 45–68. The "assumptions" are direct quotations of Berryman, but the explanations are my own commentary on Berryman's work.

False Assumption #2: Learners are passive receivers of wisdom—empty vessels into which knowledge is poured.

Each student approaches the task of learning equipped with a history— a matrix of acquired skills, knowledge, and experience—and a set of expectations and hopes. The most effective learning happens when the student is invited (and taught) to make connections between past learning and future motivations. But teaching techniques that require an essentially passive response from students, such as lecturing, deprive students of this opportunity to actively involve themselves with the material. They may miss the most important means of learning— exploration, discovery, and invention. Passive learners who are dependent upon the teacher for guidance and feedback also may fail to develop confidence in their own intuitive abilities.

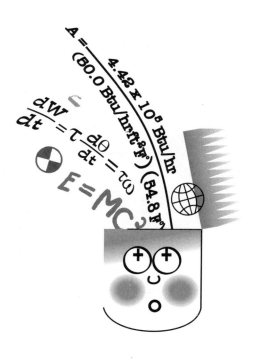

False Assumption #3: Learning is the strengthening of bonds between stimuli and correct responses.

This misconception is based on a behaviorist approach to education, which tends to reward response instead of understanding. Education based

on behaviorist theory typically leads to breaking down complex tasks and ideas into oversimplified components, unrelated subtasks, repetitive training, and an inappropriate focus on the "right answer." It does not help students learn to solve problems on a more systemic level.

False Assumption #4: What matters is getting the right answer.

Students who focus primarily on getting the right answer tend to rely on memorized shortcuts instead of acquiring the problem-solving skills they will need in a real-life setting. In the opening scenario for this chapter, for example, Tony's attention and motivation for learning are focused solely on getting the right answer. Although he may come up with the correct numbers in a classroom setting, he is not really learning the underlying concepts or how they are used in the real world.

False Assumption #5: Skills and knowledge, to be transferable to new situations, should be acquired independent of their contexts of uses.

The process of abstracting knowledge, or taking it away from its specific context, has long been thought to make that knowledge more useful to a number of situations; this philosophy underlies much of our current educational system. However, Berryman points out that such *decontextualization* can easily rob students of a sense of motivation and purpose. They may have difficulty understanding why a concept is important and how it relates to reality,

and this may make the material more difficult to retain. For example, the definition of a term may be difficult to learn and retain without understanding the context of its use.

The Context of the Workplace

In 1991, the United States Department of Labor initiated the Secretary's Commission on Achieving Necessary Skills (SCANS) to analyze the future skills that would be needed by the American workforce. The commission then prepared a report for America 2000, an initiative set up by the Bush administration to develop world-class standards for educational performance. The SCANS report reinforces the need for a more effective structure of learning that responds to the changing needs of the new workforce—and contextually based teaching methods are especially effective in making this kind of connection.

The SCANS report duly notes that traditional basic competencies such as reading, writing, and arithmetic have been and continue to be a key part of the total skills required of the workforce. However, members of the Commission strongly emphasize two other sets of competencies as critical for the current and future workforce:

- *personal qualities:* the ability to relate to others in and out of the classroom as well as developing individual responsibility and self-esteem; and

- *thinking skills:* the ability to think and problem-solve an entire system rather than working with isolated tasks and problems.

These two sets of abilities are now seen not only as skills that should be learned in combination with the three Rs, but also as the *basis* for teaching strategies that all teachers should consider using to enhance the learning capacity of their students.

The process of learning interpersonal skills, for instance, requires students to work on teams, teach others, lead, negotiate, and work well with people from culturally diverse backgrounds. But these techniques, in addition to helping students learn to get along with others, also help them learn content more effectively. The math students working together on a project not only learn interpersonal skills; they also learn *more math.*

Similarly, students acquire thinking skills best through a learning environment that requires them to be creative, make decisions, solve problems, and know how to learn and reason.[3] And once again, this kind of environment will also facilitate the learning of the course content.

The adoption of the SCANS report as a structure for learning can help students transfer knowledge from school to work and understand the context and meaning in which the curriculum is taught. It is therefore an important part of the contextual-learning model at the heart of Tech Prep/Associate Degree.

Changes in the development of the workforce require employees who have multiple skills and abilities. Similarly, the changes in the educational system must reflect the fact that students cannot continue to learn in an isolated fashion. If educational reform reshapes the way students learn, the outcome could enhance the abilities of the future workforce.

More Than One Kind of Intelligence

In a sense, there is nothing new about contextual learning. There have always been teachers who intuitively understood how to teach concepts so that all learners can grasp them—through example, illustration, and hands-on application. But even these naturally effective teachers can benefit from understanding the findings of relatively recent cognitive research and from learning how to put these findings to practical use. The results of this seminal research explain the success of contextual teaching/learning approaches in the classroom.

Cognitive science, similar in purpose and methodology to educational psychology, poses two important questions about the teaching/learning process:

- How do the human mind and body work in their learning capacity?

- How can an understanding of the mind/body's way of learning be used in educational settings?

In addressing the first question, Howard Gardner, Professor of Education at Harvard University, has challenged traditional thinking by questioning whether intelligence is a single, measurable capacity. Gardner posits instead that the human capacity for learning is much broader than traditional measurements of intelligence would indicate.

Alfred Binet, the inventor of the IQ test, standardized the assessment of intelligence through two measurements, verbal and analytical. Gardner argues, however, that individuals have as many as seven forms of intel-

---

3. Secretary's Commission on Achieving Necessary Skills, *What Work Requires of Schools: A SCANS Report for America 2000*, a letter to parents, employers, and educators (Washington, DC: Government Printing Office, 1992), 4–5.

ligence: linguistic, logical/mathematical, musical, spatial, kinesthetic, interpersonal, and intrapersonal (see figure 1). He bases this theory on his observance of the wide range of capabilities of adolescents.

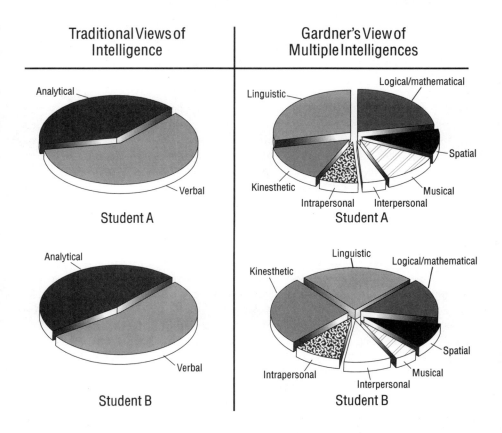

Figure 1. Traditional Versus Contemporary Views of Intelligence

For instance, Gardner describes "a fourteen-year-old adolescent in Paris, who has learned how to program a computer, is beginning to compose works of music with the aid of a synthesizer." This young Parisian displays both musical and logical/mathematical intelligence, a combination of abilities that traditional educational assessment does not usually measure or even acknowledge.

Gardner makes another important observation regarding multiple intelligences: While everyone has some measure of each of the seven intelligences, the specific strengths and combinations will vary according to the individual. No two people have the same kind of mind. (His observations of adolescents strongly support this assertion by showing that not one of the adolescents could possibly master every intelligence.) For this reason, Gardner argues against a uniform school system that does not allow students to make choices about what to learn and, even more important, how to learn.[4]

More Than One Way to Learn

Gardner's theory that individuals have multiple intelligences helps answer the second question of cognitive science—how an understanding of the mind/body's way of learning can be used in educational settings. The "learning styles" movement of the last twenty years also helps answer this question through an abundance of material it has produced concerning the various approaches students take to learning and the teaching techniques that are best suited to reaching certain students.

In his discussion of the variety of learning styles, learning theorist David Kolb observes that learners tend to perceive information either abstractly (by conceptualizing/thinking) or concretely (by experiencing/feeling) and then process that information either actively (by experimenting/doing) or reflectively (by observing/watching). Kolb, as well as other learning theorists, has typically set each of these four learning styles on an axis as a way to understand the entire realm of students' tendencies for learning.

Kolb's construction, like Gardner's, clearly indicates that most students do not fit neatly into one category or the other. Almost all students can learn by and benefit from all four experiences (thinking, feeling, doing, and watching). And no one type of learning is superior to another; all contribute to the process of effective learning. Nevertheless, most students will show a preference for one or two particular kinds of learning, and this preference will indicate the individual's primary learning style.

The emphasis for contextual learning is to use this process for effective learning to reach the strengths of all students. However, as Kolb's studies indicate, most students have a tendency to learn in a *concrete* manner (emphasis on feeling and doing), while the school system tends to teach in an *abstract* manner (emphasis on thinking and watching) as shown by the student and school house figures in figure 2.

Kolb's study of student responses found that only a small percentage of all students have a strong ability to learn by thinking and watching—the learning style catered to in the commonly used lecture method. The majority of students tend to perceive and process information through some kind of concrete experiences and/or experimentation. Most people, in other words, are *extroverted learners*; they learn best through interpersonal communication, group learning, sharing, mutual support, team processes, and positive reinforcement.

---

4. Howard Gardner, *Frames of Mind: The Theory of Multiple Intelligences* (New York: Basic Books, 1983), 4–6.

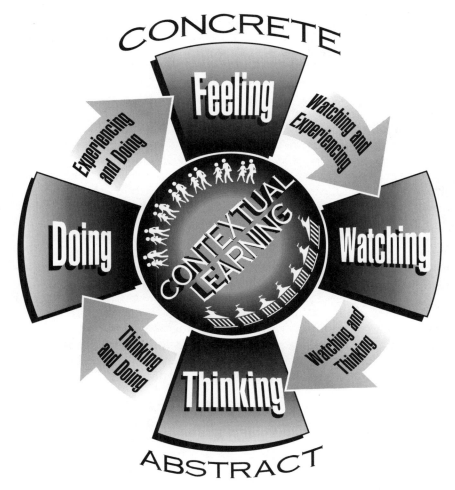

Figure 2. Contextual Learning Should Encompass All Styles of Learning.[5]

Nevertheless, Kolb encourages teaching methods to *use all* of the four styles of learning. In doing so, the student can broaden his/her learning ability beyond a natural inclination. After all, even those few students who learn best by thinking and watching eventually will be required to experience and act upon entering the workforce. And hands-on learners must be able to take the conceptual information they receive in the traditional teaching/learning methods and transfer that into practice.

---

5. Adapted from David A. Kolb, *Experiential Learning: Experience as the Source of Learning and Development* (New Jersey: Prentice-Hall, 1984).

Striving for Connectedness

Despite the individual differences in learning styles and intelligences, all learning capacities require and strive toward connectedness. Learning has a cumulative character. Isolated bits of information normally are not processed and retained by the mind for meaningful usage unless connections are made and points of reference or relationships are established between what is known and what is not known.

Teaching through illustrations and examples is a classical form of imbuing a learning experience with understanding and meaning. Many adults, for example, still remember at least one field trip or nature walk that they took in kindergarten or elementary school. The children pick up leaves or study plants and insects, learning terms and concepts while seeing and experiencing nature for themselves. Instead of just memorizing a list of names, they are allowed to touch or smell the objects that go with the names.

This concrete experience introduces meaning to the knowledge that the children are acquiring. Later they will be able to rely on their experiences and their knowledge of nature to learn more about science, the environment, and the role played by nature in literature, art, and history.

Learning theorists Renate Nummela Caine and Geoffrey Caine explain this "connectedness" theory by pointing out that all knowledge is "embedded" in other knowledge.[6] Academic "subjects" such as English, math, and chemistry are at best artificial distinctions of a single body of knowledge. Allowing these subjects to overlap and integrating them into a single curriculum can therefore provide a better, more connected understanding.

Caine and Caine suggest that any robot can be programmed to do rote memorization or acquire surface knowledge about a specific subject. However, using knowledge that a student already understands in the context or relationship of new knowledge helps the student acquire deeper understanding as well as basic facts.

In addition to making connections between different school subjects, teachers can enhance the learning process by engaging students in hands-on activities and concrete experiences as other methods to reinforce the usefulness of the knowledge. Lab activities, experiments, and projects that require students to be actively involved in the community usually stimulate interest and motivation to learn. Integrating work-based learning with school subjects is another effective way to ground learning in actual experience.

---

6. Renate Nummela Caine and Geoffrey Caine, *Making Connections: Teaching and the Human Brain* (Alexandria, VA: Association for Supervision and Curriculum Development, 1991), 92–97.

What Do We Know About the Learning Process?

The convergence of intelligence theories and learning theories suggests similar methods for more effective teaching and learning. For instance, if we accept Gardner's theory that the mind's capacity for learning is much broader than traditionally assumed, we can probably go along with Kolb's assertion that individuals have a natural ability to learn through a variety of methods. We can further conclude from the studies of Caine and Caine that connectedness is a key to effective learning. The following summary statements about effective learning are a distillation of the theories of intelligence and learning that have been addressed in this chapter:

- Most people learn best in a concrete manner involving personal participation, physical or hands-on activities, and opportunities for personal discovery.

- Learning is greatly enhanced when concepts are presented in a context of relationships that are familiar to the student.

- Most people relate better to concrete, tangible examples and experiences than to abstract conceptual models.

- The majority of students learn best through some sort of personal interaction with other students—study groups, team learning, and so on.

- Rote memorization of isolated fragments of knowledge is a relatively inefficient and ineffective learning strategy for most students.

- Transfer of learning from one situation to another is not consistently predictable, and the ability to do so is a skill in itself to be learned.

What Should Change? Some Issues for Reform

I am not qualified or sufficiently experienced in the field of learning theory to assert any absolute conclusions or definitive guidelines for the ways in which education should change to reflect current knowledge of how students learn. However, common sense raises some probing questions that suggest a rationale for the applied-academics approach that is foundational to Tech Prep/Associate Degree:

1. If only a small percentage of all students learn well through the abstract method of instruction, if that is the primary method by which most instruction is delivered in our schools, and if our national instruments of assessment are geared to measure only two out of at least seven forms of intelligence, what does this say about

the effectiveness of our primary teaching methods? Is it likely that we are reaching only a few students effectively and that we have identified these few people through the design of nationally recognized tests as our top, brightest scholars? If this is true, our public school system is at best a filter for promoting abstract learners and sending them, with honor, to the universities.

2. If we adjust our teaching styles, curricula, and testing methods to the learning styles and responses of all students, can we then expect higher achievement from nearly all students?

3. Is it important to develop multiple forms of intelligence—and abilities—in all of our students by introducing them to a variety of approaches to learning and a variety of academic environments (including contexts and applications)?

4. What are the appropriate laboratories for teaching practical applications for mathematics, science, communications, and the humanities. Can this best be accomplished through school-based labs, environmental and community-based labs, and/or work-based labs?

5. Is it reasonable to assume that nearly all students (and their parents) expect schools to prepare the students for some sort of career (life's work), and that showing the relevance between school and work (i.e. school-to-work transition) is a motivating factor and a benefit to most students?

These observations about what is happening or not happening in our schools should be quite disturbing. But what conclusions should we draw from these questions? What shape should reform take in our schools? I believe the answers to these questions point clearly toward a change in the basic way most schools do business.

In the last forty years, only a few alterations in the *content* of elementary and secondary education have been necessary. Aside from a knowledge of computers, globalization, recent history, and environmental change, students need the same sound, solid education they needed four decades ago.

Instead, the major changes needed in today's educational system center around *processes*. We need to

- provide students with compelling reasons to remain in school,

- use the discoveries of cognitive science to help them achieve enhanced learning, and

- create learning environments that open their minds and open doors for them to become more thoughtful, participative members of society and the workforce.

Clearly, if the thrust of educational reform is on the classroom (and laboratories), the emphasis should be upon empowering teachers to facilitate these processes. Karla, Tony, and Dave can be successful learners, and they can be vital elements in America's new workforce. But for this to happen on a national level, teachers like Linda must be helped to understand how students learn, teachers and students must be provided with suitable resources that also contain career-oriented motivational elements, and teachers must be provided with sufficient institutional support (including inservice training) to allow them to use new materials and equipment effectively.

Those are big "ifs," and they deserve serious discussion by educators, policymakers, and parents across the nation. But part of the good news is that appropriate materials have already been developed and are being used with over half a million students.

Thousands of teachers across the nation, particularly math and science teachers, are already experiencing unprecedented success in their classes and labs because they are being empowered to change their teaching styles. The specific courses that help them do this—materials that are squarely based on contextual learning theory and cornerstones to Tech Prep/Associate Degree reform—are known as "applied academics," and they are described in the next chapter.

4.

THE

APPLIED

**Putting Contextual
Learning to Work
in the Classroom**

ACADEMICS

APPROACH

You probably remember, as I do, one or two teachers from your school days who would use anything short of an atomic bomb to open a student's mind to the subject and skills being taught. Two teachers in particular stand out in my memory, both of them math teachers.

Their courses were not easy; in fact, they were almost painful. But even though the schoolwork seemed awfully difficult at the time, these teachers made it seem worthwhile. They were interested in me, and they understood how I learned, what I needed, and how to help me. They held up high expectations for me and would not let me compromise them. As a result, I came out of those courses with enough self-confidence and pride in myself to pursue further education. I even made it through engineering school—in part, because I was able to understand and master the math.

These are the types of teachers who are treasured by our school systems—the ones who have the natural inclination to teach to the learner. These teachers—either intuitively or intentionally—have been practicing contextual learning in their classrooms for years, although they may not have called their methods by that name. And I have no doubt that our country's school systems will always have some teachers with instincts for contextual learning.

However, there are many more teachers who have been through the traditional high school/university system and are back in the classroom teaching by the traditional methods that were taught to them—methods that are probably not the most effective for teaching the majority of students. This is not necessarily their fault; they are just part of a system that has naturally evolved. So the question then becomes: How can we change that system to empower teachers with new methods that help most students learn more efficiently?

It would be a mistake, once again, to place the burden of educational reform on the teacher and expect change to occur just because we have made teachers feel guilty or inadequate. Instead, we need to make sure that all teachers are provided with the concepts, resources, and training they need to teach most effectively. If we don't, our efforts for educational reform will stop as soon as the classroom door is shut.

Since 1985, more than 23,000 classroom doors in all fifty states have been opened to more than 650,000 students enrolled in applied-academics classes. But these are not the watered-down, low-level courses many people have come to associate with the word *applied*. These are not "dummy" classes. Today's applied-academics courses and curricula are simply academic courses and curricula with contextual teaching and learning methods built in; they team respectable academic content with a new system of instruction. The result? "It's not easy, it's just easy to learn."

The Birth of the Applied-Academics Movement

This new breed of academic instruction, which is the foundation of today's Tech Prep curriculum, began about ten years ago, when a group of educational leaders[1] met in Anaheim, California, to discuss a common dilemma in their educational institutions and especially in their high schools. These educators were concerned that most high school students taking vocational education courses had a very poor mastery of math, science, and English skills.

They knew that vocational students learned best in a hands-on or experiential manner. They also knew that students training to enter today's workforce needed "real" academic competencies, not watered-down "introductions." So they determined to form a consortium to finance and organize a science (physics) course that would teach solid academic content by means of hands-on and vocational applications.

The next few years saw the development, design, testing, and implementation of the first applied-physics course. Principles of Technology resulted from a national collaborative effort between vocational educators, academic educators (in science, mathematics, and language arts), business and

---

1. National Association of State Directors of Vocational/Technical Education Consortium (NASDVTEC), meeting with representatives of the Center for Occupational Research and Development (CORD) and the Agency for Instructional Technology (AIT) in Anaheim, CA, December 1984.

industrial representatives, and curriculum developers.[2] Its success prompted an expansion into other scientific disciplines (Applied Biology/Chemistry), plus mathematics (Applied Mathematics) and language skills (Applied Communication[3]). Later the same principles were applied by different groups to develop applied-academics curricula in humanities and economics.

The design of each curriculum required significant rearrangement (but not creation) of the academic content. To develop Principles of Technology, for instance, Leno Pedrotti and I reorganized the content of a postsecondary technical physics course around fourteen basic concepts (force, work, rate, resistance, and so on). Each concept was presented in terms of electrical, mechanical, fluid and thermal energy systems. Applied Mathematics combined concepts of prealgebra, geometry, algebra, probability/statistics and trigonometry into a single, two-course curriculum. The Applied Biology/Chemistry curriculum was designed to present both chemistry and biology in the context of common life and work experiences.

In all courses, specific applications were drawn from a variety of personal, societal, and occupational situations. All materials are suitable either for high-school students or for adults in retraining programs.

Initially, the format, presentation, and teaching strategies were based on suggestions of many teachers and on the intuitive experience of the teachers/curriculum developers. However, the sophistication of the multi-faceted learning strategies was greatly enhanced by observing ideas and guidelines from the National Council for Teachers of Mathematics, the Project 2061 report on science education, and publications of the National Science Teachers Association.

Over the past ten years, applied academics have grown from a fledgling idea to a mature curriculum that is changing the face of American education. For most schools that feature Tech Prep, applied academics are the heart and soul of the movement—and they're changing the face of American education.

Principles of Technology

Principles of Technology is a two-year applied-physics curriculum designed for tenth- and eleventh-grade students who learn more effectively with a hands-on approach (as opposed to the traditional abstract, mathematical approach). Designed to present the discipline of physics in the

---

2. The Center for Occupational Research and Development (CORD) and the Agency for Instructional Technology (AIT).

3. This curriculum was developed by the Agency for Instructional Technology.

context of how it is practically experienced in the world and how it is used in technology, Principles of Technology features:

- an integrated set of instructional materials that combines video instruction, work from printed materials, and hands-on experience;

- emphasis on the application of physics principles in mechanical, fluid, electrical, and thermal energy systems—and the analogies between these systems; and

- extensive laboratory experience, with half of the course concentrating on realistic problem-solving mathematics laboratories and hands-on hardware laboratories.

Principles of Technology covers fourteen basic technical principles (listed in figure 1) using practical language and relating these principles to specific problems. Throughout the fourteen units—seven for each year—emphasis is placed on how the principles unify an understanding of the mechanical, fluid, electrical, and thermal systems found in modern technical equipment. Teaching these principles along with the specific systems helps ensure future career flexibility, preparing students to adapt as machines and technology change and advance.

First Year	Second Year
Force	Momentum
Work	Waves
Rate	Energy Convertors
Resistance	Transducers
Energy	Radiation
Power	Optical Systems
Force Transformers	Time Constants

Figure 1. Principles of Technology Units

For students who seek to continue their education after high school, Principles of Technology provides an important academic foundation for advanced-skill classes. For students who seek immediate employment after high school, it provides a basis for understanding the job and for changing with the job. And for students who later decide to attend a four-year baccalaureate program, this course will not be wasted. More than forty universities across the nation now accept Principles of Technology as a high school laboratory-science course.

Principles of Technology was introduced in 1985. In 1993, more than 100,000 students were enrolled in Principles of Technology courses in every state in the United States and in five foreign countries.

Applied Mathematics

First introduced in the fall of 1988 and now in use by more than 180,000 students in the United States and several foreign countries, Applied Mathematics features:

- an integrated set of instructional materials that provides video instruction, work from printed materials, hands-on laboratory experience that involves extensive measurement, and practical problem-solving activities in agriculture/agribusiness, health occupations, home economics, business and marketing, and industrial technology;

- an integrated presentation of topics in arithmetic, algebra, geometry, trigonometry, probability, estimation, problem solving, and statistical process control; and

- an orientation toward application and practice of mathematics concepts and skills in the context of practical, world-of-work problems.

The thirty-six modules in Applied Mathematics are designed to be used in two one-year courses providing academic credit toward high-school graduation (see figure 2). Alternatively, separate modules can be selected as needed and infused into existing vocational courses of study. Though the units include the mathematics principles and concepts found in the traditional areas of arithmetic, geometry, algebra, simple trigonometry, and statistics, emphasis is placed squarely on the ability to understand and apply mathematics to the solution of real-world problems.

Applied Mathematics is especially helpful for students who are not necessarily baccalaureate-bound and/or those who may feel a certain anxiety about mathematics. It has been prepared for learners who have an eighth-grade prealgebra mathematics competency level and is written at the sixth- or seventh-grade reading level. Consequently, it may be used effectively— even if at a slower pace—with traditionally underserved students.

The most innovative component in the Applied Mathematics student materials is the laboratory work. Three hands-on activities are designed for each of the thirty-six modules. These activities are performed in the classroom, in the hallways, in the gymnasium, or on the school grounds and involve students in measurement and use of measuring tools. Such labs encourage students to take a participatory role in gathering and analyzing data, thereby helping them see the usefulness and applicability of mathematics in their future lives and work.

Applied Mathematics I	Applied Mathematics II
A. Getting to Know Your Calculator	16. Solving Problems That Involve Linear Equations
B. Naming Numbers in Different Ways	17. Graphing Data
C. Finding Answers with Your Calculator	18. Solving Problems That Involve Nonlinear Equations
1. Learning Problem-solving Techniques	19. Working with Statistics
2. Estimating Answers	20. Working with Probabilities
3. Measuring in English and Metric Units	21. Using Right-triangle Relationships
4. Using Graphs, Charts, and Tables	22. Using Trigonometric Functions
5. Dealing with Data	23. Factoring
6. Working with Lines and Angles	24. Patterns and Functions
7. Working with Shapes in Two Dimensions	25. Quadratics
8. Working with Shapes in Three Dimensions	26. Systems of Equations
9. Using Ratios and Proportions	27. Inequalities
10. Working with Scale Drawings	28. Geometry in the Workplace 1
11. Using Signed Numbers and Vectors	29. Geometry in the Workplace 2
12. Using Scientific Notation	30. Solving Problems with Computer Spreadsheets
13. Precision, Accuracy, and Tolerance	31. Solving Problems with Computer Graphics
14. Solving Problems with Powers and Roots	32. Quality Assurance and Process Control 1
15. Using Formulas to Solve Problems	33. Quality Assurance and Process Control 2

Figure 2. Learning Modules for Applied Mathematics

The Applied Mathematics materials fully reflect the standards set up by the National Council of Teachers of Mathematics.[4] The NCTM consensus, based on input from many math educators, is that successful completion of two years of Applied Mathematics will fulfill requirements for Algebra I and at least a half-year of informal geometry. In addition, it is their opinion that a student who successfully completes Applied Mathematics I and II can enroll in Algebra II and/or formal geometry with a reasonable expectation of success. This means the student would have the option of moving into the baccalaureate-bound mathematics sequence in the eleventh and twelfth grades with little or no backtracking.

Applied Communication

Introduced in the fall of 1988 and widely used in forty-six states, this one-year course is a resource for students that:

- teaches communication, language-arts, and English skills as they apply in the workplace,

---

4. National Council of Teachers of Mathematics, *Curriculum and Evaluation Standards for School Mathematics* (Reston, VA: National Council of Teachers of Mathematics, 1989).

- sharpens reading, writing, listening, speaking, problem-solving, visual, and nonverbal skills,

- strengthens the academic foundations of the curriculum, and

- features specific applications for the career areas of agriculture, business and marketing, health occupations, home economics, technology, and trade and industry.

Applied Communication is a comprehensive set of video-based learning materials designed to help students develop and refine job-related communication skills. The learning materials are divided into fifteen instructional modules (see figure 3) and include a total of one hundred fifty lessons.

Communicating in the Workplace	Presenting Your Point of View
Gathering and Using Information in the Workplace	Communicating with Clients and Customers
Using Problem-Solving Strategies	Making and Responding to Requests
Starting a New Job	Communicating to Solve Interpersonal Conflicts
Communicating with Co-Workers	
Participating in Groups	Evaluating Performance
Following and Giving Directions	Upgrading, Retraining, and Changing Jobs
Communicating with Supervisors	Improving the Quality of Communications

Figure 3. Learning Modules for Applied Communication

The fifteen Applied Communication modules with accompanying videos can be used singly, in any order, to enhance existing communication, language arts, English, or vocational-technical courses, or they can be used together as the basis for a one-year course. The student materials are designed for use with individuals who have at least an eighth-grade reading ability.

Applied Biology/Chemistry

The fourth applied-academics course to be developed for Tech Prep secondary students, Applied Biology/Chemistry, was introduced in 1990. By 1993, ten of the twelve designed units had been completed, enough to support up to two years of instruction; these were being used by over 30,000 students in forty-five states.

Applied Biology/Chemistry follows the same basic pedagogical model as Principles of Technology and Applied Mathematics; it features:

- an integrated set of instructional materials that provides video instruction, a student text with laboratory activities, a teacher's guide, and a resource guidebook.

- twelve units that present the scientific fundamentals of biology and chemistry and provide a foundation for careers in technology, health, agriculture/agribusiness, or home economics,

- integration of biology and chemistry as a unified domain for the purposes of teaching, and

- student activities that relate to work and other life experiences.

Applied Biology/Chemistry features an instructional system of twelve units (see figure 4). The units, each designed for fifteen to thirty hours of student activity, may be infused into existing curricula or taught together as a one- or two-year stand-alone course.

The course materials have adopted an instructional strategy recommended by the National-Science-Foundation-funded study, Project Synthesis, which emphasizes the importance of teaching science in the context of major life issues.[5] In addressing occupational, personal, and societal issues, Applied Biology/Chemistry has also followed an approach that is consistent with the National Science Teachers Association's *Criteria for Excellence.*[6] Further, the Applied Biology/Chemistry curriculum is consistent with the recommendations relative to both content and effective learning and teaching as expressed in the Project 2061 report, *Science for All Americans.*[7]

Natural Resources	Disease and Wellness
Water	Life Processes
Air and Other Gases	Synthetic Materials
Plant Growth and Reproduction	Waste and Waste Management
Continuity of Life	Microorganisms
Nutrition	Community of Life

Figure 4. Learning Modules for Applied Biology/Chemistry

5. N. C. Harms and R. E. Yager, eds., *What Research Says to the Science Teacher*, vol. 3 (Washington, DC: National Science Teachers Association, 1987).

6. National Science Teachers Association, *Criteria for Excellence* (Washington, DC: National Science Teachers Association, 1987).

7. American Association for the Advancement of Science, *Science for All Americans: A Project 2061 Report on Literacy Goals in Science, Mathematics and Technology* (Washington, DC: American Association for the Advancement of Science, 1989).

Applied Humanities

Seattle Community College of Seattle, Washington, in conjunction with the Boeing Company, is in the process of developing an Applied Humanities curriculum. It is divided into four individual units or courses.

- Critical Thinking and Ethics in the Workplace (Applied Philosophy)

- Responsibilities and Rights of Citizenship (Applied Civics)

- Life Cycles of Business, Products, and Technologies (Applied History)

- Industrial Design and Human Factors (Applied Art)

Some of these courses are still in a formative stage at this writing and distribution will therefore be limited before 1991–1994. Nevertheless, they show the potential of contextual learning methods when applied to a wide variety of subjects.

Critical Thinking and Ethics in the Workplace (Applied Philosophy)

This course provides an introduction to critical thinking, logic, and scientific reasoning with applications to other courses, everyday life, and work. It has been created with technical education students in mind; whenever possible, topics are related directly to the programs of study and the future careers of technical education students.

Responsibilities and Rights of Citizenship (Applied Civics)

This course examines rights and responsibilities in a free society in the practical context of an individual's roles as a citizen, family member, and employee or employer. The course distinguishes between legally enforceable rights and obligations and those rights and responsibilities that are considered essential to a free society. The course is designed to assist students in thinking clearly about these issues and to add a dimension of values to the process as well.

Life Cycles of Business, Products, and Technologies (Applied History)

This course enables students to use the content, analytical processes, research methods, analytic methods, and writing techniques of history to anticipate, understand, and benefit from changing technologies. The course also provides students with insight into the ongoing processes of business, industrial, and technological change that have affected them as consumers and will continue to affect them as workers.

Industrial Design and Human Factors (Applied Art)

This course assists students in developing an aesthetic approach to technology and the world of work. The aesthetic concepts of quality, beauty, good design, and an effective work environment are explored from a variety of viewpoints, including the philosophical, multicultural, psychological, economic, and technological. The course covers such topics as aesthetic values, the psychology of perception, social values, economics and design, production and materials, and vocational applications.

Applied Economics

Yet another highly effective applied-academics course has been developed by the National Headquarters for Junior Achievement, Incorporated. Applied Economics is a one-semester class that has been implemented in almost every state. In nineteen states, Applied Economics has been recommended for adoption as either a required economics credit or an elective.

The Applied Economics program is designed to:

- describe the basic characteristics of the American economic system, with emphasis on the roles of private property, the price system, and competition;

- demonstrate how fundamental economic concepts such as markets, economic incentives, and opportunity cost operate in the American and other economic systems;

- develop students' understanding of the economic principles that influence business decisions;

- help students grasp the economic roles governments play in a market economy;

- show the need for ethical standards in business leaders, producers, and consumers;

- foster appropriate life, study, and decision-making skills;

- enable students to explore career opportunities, consumer issues, and other aspects of personal economics;

- provide "hands-on" experiences in the operation of a business enterprise;

- provide opportunities for students to interact with representatives of the business community.

This last feature has been an integral part of the success of the Applied Economics course. Through the help of the local Junior Achievement offices, teachers and local business representatives are trained to work together as a team to teach the course. In a typical week, the teacher will work with the class for four days, and the business representative will teach the fifth day. The result is a class that is solidly grounded in both sound economic theory and real-world application.

Where Do the Applied Math and Science Curricula Fit in a TPAD Program?

Figure 5 shows a partial distribution of courses or course sequences generally required for high school graduation and suggests a possible sequence of applied-academics courses. Several observations relative to this suggested course of study are in order.

	9th Grade	10th Grade	11th Grade	12th Grade
MATH	Applied Math I	Applied Math II	Algebra II	Formal Geometry
SCIENCE	Applied Biology/ Chemistry	Principles of Technology I	Principles of Technology II (Optional)	
ENGLISH	English I, II, and III and Applied Communication			
SOCIAL STUDIES	Geography, History, and Government			
OTHER			Vocational Education Concentration	Vocational Education Concentration

Figure 5. Applied Academics in a Four-Year High School Program

First, in the mathematics sequence, Applied Mathematics I and II are to be taken in the ninth and tenth grades, respectively. Inclusion of Applied Mathematics in the first two years of high school provides technical students with a sound, functional foundation in mathematics that will serve them in the technical courses to follow. At the same time, taking Applied Mathematics in the first two years of high school keeps the students' options open.

Those who change career plans and decide to pursue a four-year college degree can then enter the traditional, baccalaureate-bound mathematics sequence, taking Algebra II in the junior year and a higher-level geometry or precalculus course in the senior year. Selection and satisfactory completion of these follow-on courses will enable students to meet most college-entrance requirements in mathematics.

In the science sequence, Applied Biology/Chemistry is suggested for the ninth grade, with Principles of Technology I following in the tenth grade and—if time permits—Principles of Technology II or another science course in the eleventh or twelfth grade.

It is important to note at this point that students who take Applied Mathematics in the ninth grade are more likely to complete Principles of Technology in the tenth or eleventh grade with a high degree of success. And again, an increasing number of four-year colleges and universities now accept Principles of Technology as an entrance requirement for laboratory science. This benefits those students who take Principles of Technology in high school and subsequently decide to enter a four-year college program.

The sequence of four English courses generally required in our high schools has been modified to make room for one year of Applied Communication. Different states are trying Applied Communication at different grade levels, and some are infusing Applied Communication modules into English courses during all four high school years. I have therefore left its specific position in the curriculum up to administration and teachers in the local school districts.

The "Other" category has purposefully been left open. Different schools and different states have differing graduation requirements that generally will be included in this area. For Tech Prep students, however, it is vital to include concentration in a "technical cluster" area in the junior and senior years. (A technical cluster is a group of careers that require similar basic training.)

The specific area of concentration—whether transportation, health occupations, electronics, manufacturing, human services, construction techniques, or another field—is less important than the practice and learning of valuable hand skills that are acquired through technical courses. To provide students with applied-academics courses and deprive them of associated hand-skill training in technical areas would be to do them an injustice. Fortunately, in most Tech Prep programs, concentration in a technical area in the high school is already built-in as part of the curriculum.

How Applied Academics Put Learning in Context

The applied-academics curricula described in this chapter have been deliberately designed to incorporate as many facets of contextual learning as possible. As chapter 3 explains, these facets include relating, transferring, applying, experiencing, and cooperating.

Relating

Learning in the context of life experience, or *relating*, is the kind of contextual learning that typically occurs with very young children. For toddlers, the sources of learning are readily at hand in the form of toys, games, and everyday events such as meals, trips to the grocery, and walks in the neighborhood.

As children grow older, however, providing this meaningful context for learning becomes more difficult. Ours is a society in which the workplace is largely separated from residential life, in which extended families are separated by great distances, and in which teens lack a clear societal role or responsibilities commensurate with their abilities.

Under ideal conditions, teachers might simply lead students from one community-based activity to another, encouraging them to relate what they are learning to real-life experience. In most cases, however, given the range and complexity of concepts to be taught and the limitations of our resources, life experiences will have to be evoked through text, video, speech, and classroom activity.

The curriculum that attempts to place learning in the context of life experiences needs first to call the student's attention to everyday sights, events, and conditions and then to link these everyday situations to new information to be absorbed or a problem to be solved. This is precisely the approach that applied-academics courses take.

In Principles of Technology, for example, the unit on momentum uses the familiar experience of driving a car and the common knowledge of what happens in an automobile collision to help students relate two basic physics concepts, impulse and change in momentum, to everyday life. As these concepts are introduced, students are first reminded of a moving car and encouraged to think of their own experience as drivers or passengers. Then the class goes on to discuss the motion of a human body in a moving car as it slams into a guard rail. The connection is made between this collision and the concept of impulse (a force acting for a period of time).

From this point, the student is led from very familiar sights and events (a car collision) to understand a phenomenon that is more difficult to observe: change in momentum. This is done by introducing an air bag between the driver and the dashboard. Because the air bag increases the length of time during impact, it decreases the amount of force exerted by the driver's body and thus reduces injury.

Finally, having understood momentum in the context of an automobile crash, the student is helped to relate the same concepts to other life experiences—for instance, the planned collision of a massive wrecking ball, the follow-through of a golf swing or tennis stroke, or the forces given a bullet fired from a rifle.

Large forces acting for a *short time* can cause damage to a dashboard—or to a human

Fig. 8-8 Momentum and a planned collision.

...nplanned collision.

Fig. 8-10 Impulse in sports.

Figure 6. Automobile Collisions and Golf Relate to a Change in Momentum.

In another Principles of Technology unit, a laboratory in which students are to measure the impact force of water in a pipe is introduced by asking students to recall a common experience—the sound of "water hammer," or the noise that water pipes sometimes make when they are turned off quickly. The experience of water hammer is linked to a sudden change in pressure, or a pressure spike. This in turn leads to a discussion of momentum and eventually to the measurement of fluid velocity in the laboratory and the calculation of momentum.

...ve a momentum cha...
These vehicles leave the ground and then return with a great deal of momentum. (See Figure 1.) The downward momentum must be brought to

Regular bumper

Figure 7. Five-Mile-Per-Hour Bumpers Relate the Ideas of Impulse and Change of Momentum.

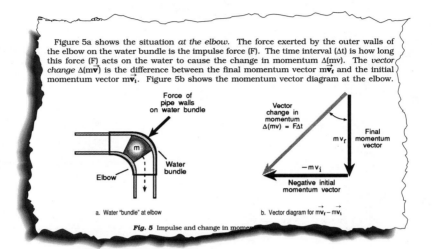

Figure 5a shows the situation *at the elbow*. The force exerted by the outer walls of the elbow on the water bundle is the impulse force (F). The time interval (Δt) is how long this force (F) acts on the water to cause the change in momentum Δ(mv). The *vector change* Δ(m**v**) is the difference between the final momentum vector m**v**$_f$ and the initial momentum vector m**v**$_i$. Figure 5b shows the momentum vector diagram at the elbow.

a. Water "bundle" at elbow

b. Vector diagram for m**v**$_f$ − m**v**$_i$

Fig. 5 Impulse and change in momentum

Figure 8. Forces Caused by Fluids Turning a Corner in a Pipe Can Be Analyzed With Vectors.

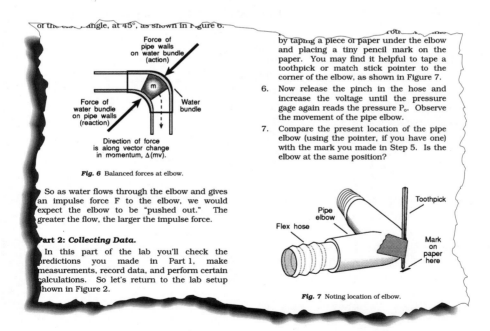

of the elbow, at 45°, as shown in Figure 6.

Fig. 6 Balanced forces at elbow.

So as water flows through the elbow and gives an impulse force F to the elbow, we would expect the elbow to be "pushed out." The greater the flow, the larger the impulse force.

Part 2: *Collecting Data.*

In this part of the lab you'll check the predictions you made in Part 1, make measurements, record data, and perform certain calculations. So let's return to the lab setup shown in Figure 2.

by taping a piece of paper under the elbow and placing a tiny pencil mark on the paper. You may find it helpful to tape a toothpick or match stick pointer to the corner of the elbow, as shown in Figure 7.

6. Now release the pinch in the hose and increase the voltage until the pressure gage again reads the pressure P$_o$. Observe the movement of the pipe elbow.

7. Compare the present location of the pipe elbow (using the pointer, if you have one) with the mark you made in Step 5. Is the elbow at the same position?

Fig. 7 Noting location of elbow.

Figure 9. Fluids Moving Around Sharp Pipe Bends Undergo Changes in Momentum That Result in Forces on the Pipe.

In a similar learning path, students begin the unit on quadratic equations in Applied Mathematics with illustrations of two very familiar objects with parabolic shapes—a flashlight with its curved reflector and a television satellite dish. These everyday objects precede the discussion of conic sections and the presentation of equations. Students are thus led to relate something from within their experience (the flashlight or satellite dish) to something unknown (a mathematical equation that expresses the familiar shape).

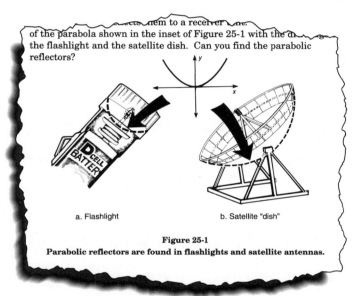

...ects them to a receiver ...v.
of the parabola shown in the inset of Figure 25-1 with the d...
the flashlight and the satellite dish. Can you find the parabolic reflectors?

a. Flashlight   b. Satellite "dish"

Figure 25-1
Parabolic reflectors are found in flashlights and satellite antennas.

Figure 10. The Mathematics Behind Parabolas Can Be Related to Everyday Uses Such as the Flashlight and Satellite Dish.

The evocation of the familiar may be achieved through many techniques, including student activities, video, or even a dramatic narrative. Examples of both can be found in the Applied Biology/Chemistry unit on nutrition, in which students learn that they really are what they eat.

In a potentially intimidating section on the chemistry of various foods, for instance, students are introduced to the primary nutrients (water, carbohydrates, lipids, protein, vitamins, and minerals) through a narrative about an overweight teenager. The narrative is helpful in motivating students and informing them about the importance of understanding these nutrients in order to evaluate a diet. But the students are really encouraged to relate the study of nutrients to their own lives through activities such as the one that asks them to form groups, select a fast-food restaurant, and then analyze the protein-to-fat and protein-to-carbohydrate ratios in a typical meal. In keeping with good learning theory, the point of departure is the learner herself (or himself) and that most universal of human experiences—eating.

Finally, Samantha consulted a doctor to see if she has some physiological problem that causes her to gain more readily than other people. The doctor found no such problem and referred Samantha to Melanie for nutritional counseling. "Starving yourself is not the answer to any weight problem," Melanie explains. "Before we do anything, Samantha, let's try to get a realistic idea of what you eat now. I'd like you to keep a diary for the next week."

"A diary?" asks Samantha.

"A food diary," answers Melanie. "A record of everything you eat and drink (including water) at meals and between meals. And please record the time that you eat."

"Oh this is going to be embarrass...

Figure 11. Biology and Chemistry Can Relate to a Student's Personal Fears Such as a Weight Problem.

ACTIVITY 2-7

Many teenagers prefer fast food to eating at home. You may be one of those who would rather have a pizza or a quick burger meal than the sit-down meals served at home. Now that you've learned about carbohydrates, fats, and proteins, you can find out what's really in a fast-food meal.

- Form small groups of four or five people in each group.
- As a group, select a different fast-food restaurant that you like, such as McDonald's, Kentucky Fried Chicken, etc.
- Using nutrition tables provided by your teacher, analyze the protein-to-fat and protein-to-carbohydrate ratio in a typical meal at the selected restaurant.
- Compare you findings with those of others in the class and answer the following questions:
  1. Which fast-food meal contains the greatest amount of fat?
  2. Which meal contains the greatest amount of protein?
  3. Which fast-food meal contains the highest protein-to-fat ratio?
  4. Which meal contains the highest carbohydrate-to-protein ratio?

Figure 12. Biology and Chemistry Students Analyze the Nutrition in Fast-Food Meals.

Transferring

Learning in the context of existing knowledge, or transferring, uses and builds upon what the student already knows. Such an approach is similar to relating in that it calls upon the familiar.

As adults, many of us are adept at avoiding situations that are unfamiliar—the part of town we don't know, the unusual food we've never eaten, the store we haven't shopped. Sometimes we also avoid situations in which we have to gain new information or develop a new skill (especially if there are likely to be witnesses)—using a new type of computer software or coping in another country with our fledgling foreign-language skills.

High school students, however, rarely have the luxury of ducking out of new learning situations; they are confronted with them every day. We can help them retain their sense of dignity and develop confidence if we make a point of building new learning experiences on what they already know.

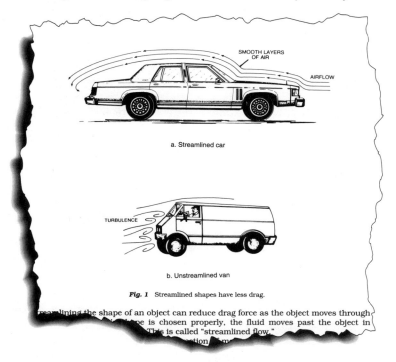

a. Streamlined car

b. Unstreamlined van

Fig. 1 Streamlined shapes have less drag.

reamlining the shape of an object can reduce drag force as the object moves through e is chosen properly, the fluid moves past the object in This is called "streamlined flow."

Figure 13. Students Transfer Knowledge of "Drag" to Understand the Reasons for Drag Resistance.

An example of transferring or building on students' prior knowledge is found in the Principles of Technology subunit on resistance in mechanical systems. Students' intuitive knowledge of "drag" and familiarity with the concept of streamlining in automobile design are drawn out in a prelab discussion of drag force, airflow, and turbulence. In the laboratory exercise that follows, students will measure the airflow past three test objects, thus verifying their intuitive understanding.

the force indicated on the spring and record value in the appropriate in the Data Table.
dually increase the voltage in one-volt to 12 volts. At each voltage setting

object. Repeat Steps 4 through 6.
▲*CAUTION: Do not exchange tes jects while fan is ru*
If you drop the test you will ruin fan bla

DATA TABLE: DRAG FORCE DUE TO AIRFLOW PAST TEST OBJECT

Test Object	Voltage Applied to Fan				
	8 V	9 V	10 V	11 V	12 V
Disk Shape					
Cone Shape					
Optional Shape					

Figure 14. Students Measure Drag Forces on Differently Shaped Objects.

Sometimes students have knowledge of which they are not aware, simply because what they know has not been called to their attention or named or otherwise given a value. For example, a boy or girl who has learned to make minor bicycle repairs knows something about belt drives. Chances are that no one has pointed out to the budding bicycle mechanic that he or she therefore possesses a practical knowledge of force transformation, but the knowledge is there nonetheless. To begin a subunit on force transformers with an illustration of a bicycle belt drive, as the Principles of Technology course does, is to show the student that he or she has knowledge already and to prepare him or her to use that knowledge.

Applied-academics courses often encourage students to reflect on what they know about a subject before they begin a sequence of study. In an Applied Communication module on communicating with clients and customers, for example, students examine a series of photographs that show two people, a parent and a day-care worker, interacting. Students are asked to identify the feelings and attitudes of each person toward the other and to reflect on the importance of nonverbal behaviors in the resolution of the exchange. This exercise helps the students become aware of their own prior knowledge of nonverbal communication and thus prepares them to read a text discussion of nonverbal behaviors and to carry out an observation exercise.

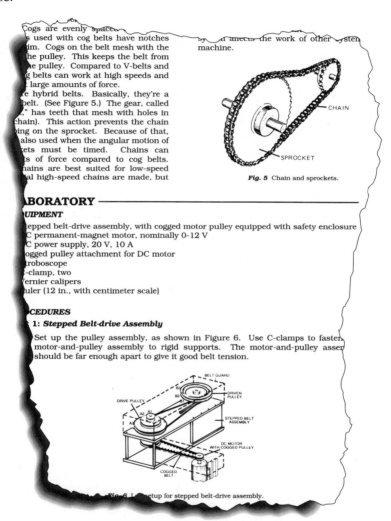

Cogs are evenly spaced ...
s used with cog belts have notches ... im. Cogs on the belt mesh with the ... he pulley. This keeps the belt from ... he pulley. Compared to V-belts and ... g belts can work at high speeds and ... large amounts of force.
... e hybrid belts. Basically, they're a ... belt. (See Figure 5.) The gear, called ..., " has teeth that mesh with holes in ... chain). This action prevents the chain ... ing on the sprocket. Because of that, ... also used when the angular motion of ... ets must be timed. Chains can ... s of force compared to cog belts. ... hains are best suited for low-speed ... al high-speed chains are made, but

... ay ... affects the work of other ... stem machine.

Fig. 5 Chain and sprockets.

BORATORY

UIPMENT

epped belt-drive assembly, with cogged motor pulley equipped with safety enclosure
C permanent-magnet motor, nominally 0-12 V
C power supply, 20 V, 10 A
ogged pulley attachment for DC motor
troboscope
-clamp, two
ernier calipers
uler (12 in., with centimeter scale)

CEDURES

1: *Stepped Belt-drive Assembly*

Set up the pulley assembly, as shown in Figure 6. Use C-clamps to fasten motor-and-pulley assembly to rigid supports. The motor-and-pulley asser should be far enough apart to give it good belt tension.

Fig. 6 ... etup for stepped belt-drive assembly.

Figure 15. Students Transfer Knowledge of Bicycle Chains to Work With Mechanical Force Transformers in the Laboratory.

worker?

- What are the feelings and attitudes of the parent in the earlier pictures? In the later pictures?

- What is the attitude of the day-care worker toward the parent? What evidence supports your conclusion?

- Does the situation appear to be resolved in the final photographs? How can you tell?

- In your opinion, what nonverbal behaviors were imprtant in the exchange? Why?

Figure 16. Students Learn How to Communicate with Clients and Customers.

In some cases, building on what a student "knows" is actually a matter of exposing opinion or misconception. For example, a subunit on genetic inheritance in the Applied Biology/Chemistry course includes a scenario in which a married couple visits a genetic counselor because they are both carriers of sickle-cell genes and are concerned about the health of any children they might have. The scenario identifies genetic terminology such as *recessive*, *dominant*, and *heterozygous* and introduces the Punnett square used as a tool by genetic science.

In this case, students may or may not know a great deal about sickle-cell anemia. Chances are good that they have heard of it, but they are also likely to have fears and misconceptions about it. The text and the teacher can use what students "know"—that is, all that they have heard or believe about sickle-cell anemia—to propel them into a learning experience. Thus, the transference can take place whether or not the students' original conceptions were accurate.

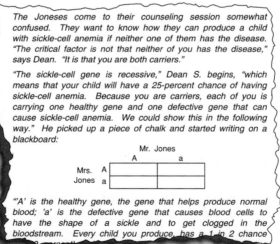

Figure 17. Students Transfer Familiarity With a Common Disease
to a Lesson on Genes.

Applying

Contextual learning of the relating and transferring varieties asks students to call upon past and present experiences that have occurred or are occurring in an environment with which they are familiar. By contrast, *applying* concepts and information in a useful context often projects students into an imagined future (a possible career) and/or into an unfamiliar location (a workplace). In the applied-academics courses, applications are often based on occupational activities.

Young people today generally lack access to the workplace; unlike members of previous generations, they do not see the modern-day counterpart to the blacksmith at the forge or the farmers in the field. Essentially ghettoized in the inner city or outer suburbia, many students have a greater knowledge of how to become a rock star or a model than of how to become a respiratory therapist or a power plant operator. If they are to get a realistic sense of connection between schoolwork and real-life jobs, therefore, the occupational context must be brought to them. This happens most commonly through text, video, labs, and activities, although in many

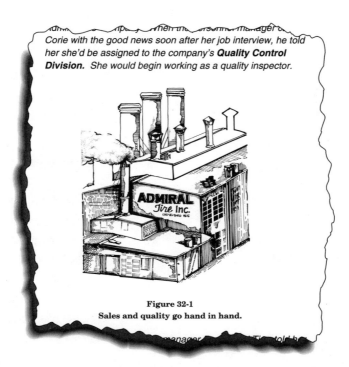

Corie with the good news soon after her job interview, he told her she'd be assigned to the company's **Quality Control Division.** She would begin working as a quality inspector.

Figure 32-1
Sales and quality go hand in hand.

Figure 18. Students Apply "Austere" Mathematics Concepts to a Work Environment.

schools, these contextual learning experiences will be followed up with firsthand experiences such as plant tours, mentoring arrangements, and internships.

Applying academic concepts in an occupational context helps give purpose and importance to what might otherwise appear to the student as meaningless exercises. For example, the Applied Mathematics unit on Quality Assurance and Process Control begins with a narrative about Corie, a newly hired quality inspector for a tire company. The story makes clear that Corie will be using mathematical concepts such as standard deviations, mean values, and data spread to carry out significant responsibilities within the company. Further discussion of quality control helps to motivate and prepare the student to eventually tackle more sophisticated techniques of data analysis.

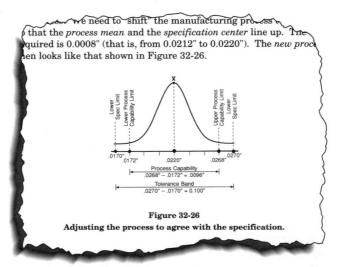

...we need to shift the manufacturing process so that the *process mean* and the *specification center* line up. The required is 0.0008" (that is, from 0.0212" to 0.0220"). The *new process* then looks like that shown in Figure 32-26.

Figure 32-26
Adjusting the process to agree with the specification.

Figure 19. Students Can Apply Statistics to the Quality of Production in the Workplace.

The introduction of new concepts in a workplace context also helps students to overcome their unfamiliarity by giving them a meaningful application. In the Applied Biology/Chemistry course, for instance, students are introduced to molar and normal solutions through a narrative called "Condition Red!" in which a chemical technician in a textile factory discovers that the concentration of dye in the plant effluent has exceeded EPA standards. Based on a true story told by the featured technician (as are most of the scenarios in the Applied Biology/Chemistry course), the scenario effectively introduces the concept of concentration in a graphic and memorable way.

Condition Red!

Yvonne Ybarra is having an off-day at the textile plant, no, make that an off-week. Her job is to monitor the water quality of all of the water used in the plant's production processes. She also oversees the quality of water released by the plant into the nearby river; this outgoing water is known as effluent.

Yvonne has to make regular reports to the Environmental Protection Agency (EPA) and other government agencies. However, these agencies don't just take Yvonne's word for it when it comes to water quality; they also monitor the quality of the river water at regular intervals.

This week Yvonne has a quarterly report due to the EPA; she also has some reports to make to the plant manager. So the last thing she needs is a complication, but that's just what she's got. The plant effluent is showing a higher concentration of residual dye than is acceptable to return to the river. The effluent meets EPA standards, but it doesn't

Figure 20. Environmental Hazards Are Applied to Biology and Chemistry.

ompound, simply weigh in grams one formula weight. Recall from subunit 1 that the formula weight is the sum of the atomic weights e elements in the molecular formula. To get those atomic weights, u will need to use the periodic table (Figure 3-7).

Suppose you needed to make a one molar solution of sodium bicarbonate ($NaHCO_3$).

- First, you need the formula weight of sodium bicarbonate, which you can find by consulting the periodic table and adding the atomic weights of each element in the molecular formula $NaHCO_3$, $23 + 1 + 12 + (16 \times 3) = 84$ grams per mole. This tells you that it takes 84 grams of $NaHCO_3$ to make a one molar solution of sodium bicarbonate.
- You then weigh 84 grams of sodi

Figure 21. After Seeing the Application of Concentration in Condition Red, Students Learn How to Work the Calculations.

Job-related applications in applied-academics courses may be based on actual occupational activities, but they may also be based on devices and systems used in occupational or other settings. In a Principles of Technology subunit on resistance in thermal systems, for example, students make measurements, collect data, and perform calculations to determine the thermal resistance in an insulated chamber. Their laboratory setup for this exercise mimics the basic components of many industrial devices in which insulation is required, and the lab is preceded by examples of two such devices: an air intake heater from a coal-fired power plant and a solar collector. The laboratory activity thus becomes believable and valuable to students because it is related to real work. Students also become aware that such devices actually exist outside the world of school, and they realize implicitly that someone must install, monitor, and maintain these devices.

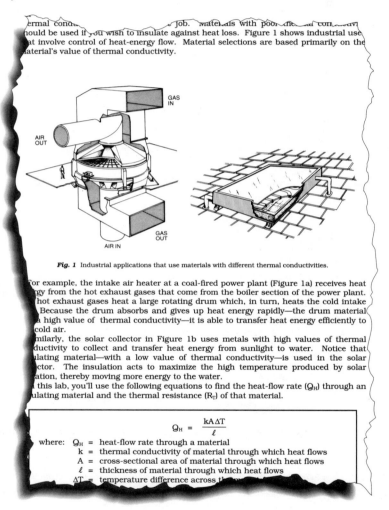

ermal condu_____ job. mate____als with poor___ne____al con___av]
hould be used if you wish to insulate against heat loss. Figure 1 shows industrial use
at involve control of heat-energy flow. Material selections are based primarily on the
aterial's value of thermal conductivity.

Fig. 1 Industrial applications that use materials with different thermal conductivities.

or example, the intake air heater at a coal-fired power plant (Figure 1a) receives heat
gy from the hot exhaust gases that come from the boiler section of the power plant.
hot exhaust gases heat a large rotating drum which, in turn, heats the cold intake
Because the drum absorbs and gives up heat energy rapidly—the drum material
a high value of thermal conductivity—it is able to transfer heat energy efficiently to
cold air.
milarly, the solar collector in Figure 1b uses metals with high values of thermal
ductivity to collect and transfer heat energy from sunlight to water. Notice that
lating material—with a low value of thermal conductivity—is used in the solar
ctor. The insulation acts to maximize the high temperature produced by solar
ation, thereby moving more energy to the water.
this lab, you'll use the following equations to find the heat-flow rate (Q_H) through an
ulating material and the thermal resistance (R_T) of that material.

$$Q_H = \frac{kA\,\Delta T}{\ell}$$

where: Q_H = heat-flow rate through a material
         k = thermal conductivity of material through which heat flows
         A = cross-sectional area of material through which heat flows
         ℓ = thickness of material through which heat flows
         ΔT = temperature difference across th___

Figure 22. Students Apply Physics Equations to Industrial Uses.

Applying learning in the context of how knowledge can be used does not always focus on occupations, however. Sometimes personal and societal problems provide a context for the knowledge and skills required to solve them. For example, the unit on Air in Applied Biology/Chemistry features a description of the disastrous industrial accident at Bhopal in 1984. The scenario introduces several crucial societal issues, including worker safety, environmental pollution, and the need for increased self-regulation in the chemical industry. It also emphasizes to students that the concepts of density, molecular weight, and diffusion that follow are far from trivial or abstract; they are the factors that must be considered in order to assess the dispersion effects of a harmful gas.

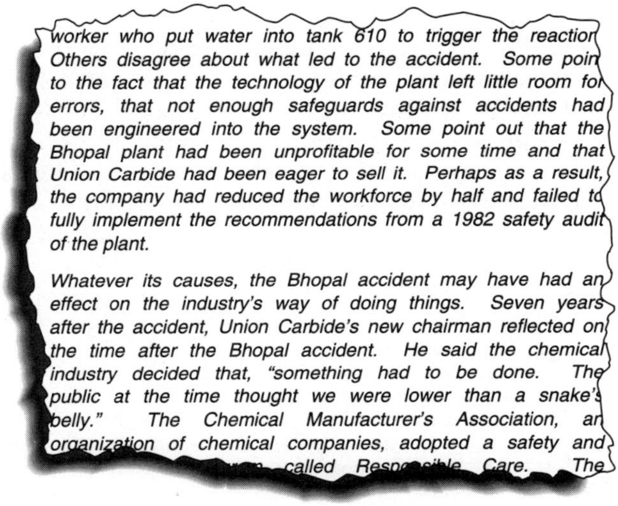

worker who put water into tank 610 to trigger the reaction. Others disagree about what led to the accident. Some point to the fact that the technology of the plant left little room for errors, that not enough safeguards against accidents had been engineered into the system. Some point out that the Bhopal plant had been unprofitable for some time and that Union Carbide had been eager to sell it. Perhaps as a result, the company had reduced the workforce by half and failed to fully implement the recommendations from a 1982 safety audit of the plant.

Whatever its causes, the Bhopal accident may have had an effect on the industry's way of doing things. Seven years after the accident, Union Carbide's new chairman reflected on the time after the Bhopal accident. He said the chemical industry decided that, "something had to be done. The public at the time thought we were lower than a snake's belly." The Chemical Manufacturer's Association, an organization of chemical companies, adopted a safety and called Responsible Care. The

Figure 23. Biology and Chemistry Are Applied to Societal Issues.

Experiencing

Experiencing—learning in the context of exploration, discovery, and invention—is the heart of the applied-academics curricula. However motivated or tuned-in students may become as a result of other instructional strategies such as video, narrative, or text-based activities, these remain relatively passive forms of contextual learning. And learning appears to "take" far more quickly when students are able to manipulate equipment and materials and to do other forms of active research.

In applied-academics courses, the laboratories are often based on actual workplace tasks. The point here is not to train students for specific jobs, but to allow them to experience activities that have a direct relationship to real-life work. However, many of the activities and skills selected for labs are cross-disciplinary; that is, they are used in a broad spectrum of occupations.

One particular activity in an Applied Mathematics unit on using the calculator provides a good example of how experiencing enforces learning. Students are required to follow a set of written instructions to determine the amount of pipe needed to run a temporary cold-water pipe from one specified location to another and to determine the material costs of running the pipe. The most obvious context for this activity is the plumbing trade; however, the skills used—following directions, measuring, pricing, calculating, and reporting—are used in a wide variety of occupations.

This activity has an added dimension because the students are asked to improve upon the original statement of the problem by rewriting the instructions as they would be written for an employee. Pairs of students then exchange sets of instructions and each individual works from his or her partner's written directions; in effect, each student becomes the employer and the employee of another student. What might have been an isolated exercise in measuring or calculating or following (and writing) instructions has therefore become a workplace simulation involving many components that the student must learn to sort out. This activity is truly experiential; it involves discovery, exploration and invention on the part of the student.

...s die. A straw h...

sperm cells if the artificial insemination is to be successful. Otherwise, you, the rancher, will have to wait another three to four weeks for your cow to come back into estrous and be reinseminated. Because this loss of time delays the birth of a calf, you will have lost valuable time for beef production. In addition you have lost money paid for semen and for vet services.

Safety Precautions

- Be careful in handling objects frozen in nitrogen vapor. They are extremely cold and may give you frostbite.

Method

Part I. Thawing Semen in a Thermos

You will work in pairs.

1. Adjust the hot and cold running water on your tap until the water is 95-98°F. Fill the straw thermos with the 95-98°F tap water and cover the thermos with its lid.

2. Do the following without delay in between steps:

   - **Put on the cloth gloves and goggles.** Using tweezers put a metal cane far enough out of the tank to expose the top row of straws. **The metal canes are extremely cold—do not**

Figure 24. Students Test the Viability of Bull Semen for Artificial Insemination Through a Practice Done by Many Cattle Ranchers.

Experiential learning takes events and concepts out of the realm of abstract thought and brings them into the realm of concrete exploration. As students begin to develop a repertoire of such experiences, they develop both skills and confidence in their ability to handle (literally and figuratively) the challenges of the world outside of school.

In applied academics, the appeal of hands-on activities is often enhanced by a "you are there" approach. For instance, an Applied Biology/Chemistry lab addresses the student like this, "You are a cattle rancher with a cow in estrus. You have just received your shipment of frozen semen from a bull that has qualities you would like to breed into your stock. The sperm was shipped to you . . ." The lab goes on to instruct students to compare the viability of actual bull semen samples and to evaluate the effect of handling procedures on sperm viability.

These activities provide students with opportunities for exploration and discovery that can be applied in many situations beyond the single agricultural skill that is addressed directly. As they successfully complete this exercise, for example, students gain confidence that can be applied to handling any biological specimen or transferred to other types of materials handling. In addition, as they observe how their techniques of handling bull semen affect sperm viability, they will gain a deeper understanding of how processes can affect outcomes in any situation.

Similarly, in the previously mentioned Principles of Technology laboratory on thermal resistance, students experience working with several types of instrumentation: they mount thermocouples, read thermometers, set the voltage on a power supply, record voltage readings, and calculate thermal resistance. By performing these tasks, they not only learn the principles of resistance in thermal systems; they also gain confidence in handling and reading instrumentation, in gathering data, and in making calculations.

Cooperating

Learning in the context of sharing, responding, and communicating with other learners—or cooperating—is a primary instructional strategy in applied-academics courses. The experience of cooperating not only helps the majority of students learn the material; it is also consistent with the occupational focus of applied academics.

Research interviews with employers reveal that employees who can communicate effectively, who share information freely, and who can work comfortably in a team setting are highly valued in the workplace. We have ample reason, therefore, to encourage students to develop these cooperative skills while they are still in the classroom.

The laboratory, one of the primary instructional methods in applied academics, is essentially cooperative in its nature. Typically, students work with partners to do the laboratory exercises; in some cases, they work in groups of three or four. Completing the lab successfully requires delegation, observation, suggestion, and discussion. In many labs, the quality of the data collected by the team as a whole is dependent on the performance of each individual member of the team.

During an Applied Biology/Chemistry lab in the Disease and Wellness unit, for example, students simulate the spreading of a disease by transferring solutions from one test tube to another. Two stock solutions are used—an acid, which represents a non-disease-carrying fluid, and a base, which represents a disease-carrying fluid. Subsequent pH testing with a substance called phenol red indicates which students contracted the "disease" by coming in contact with the acid solution. By working together, the class traces the "disease" to its original "carriers." In the process, they learn correct lab techniques (pipetting, mixing solutions, pH testing) and proper ways of recording data (the "disease contacts" and the occurrences of contacts).

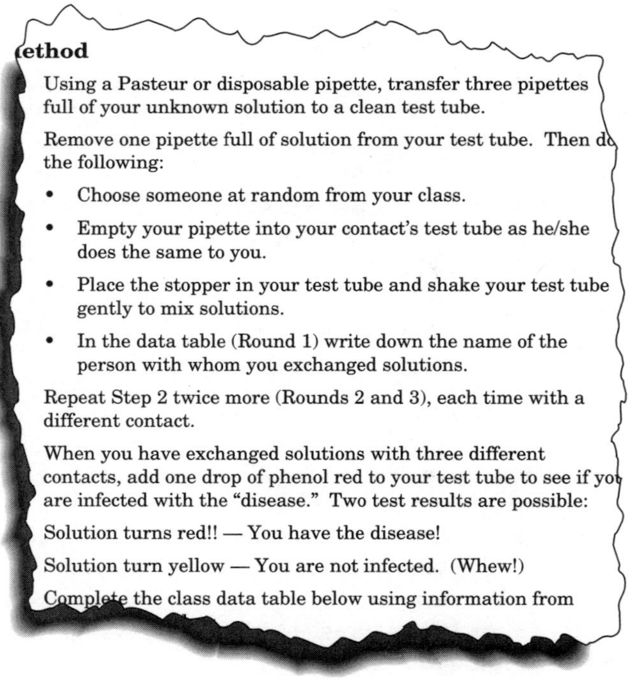

Method

Using a Pasteur or disposable pipette, transfer three pipettes full of your unknown solution to a clean test tube.

Remove one pipette full of solution from your test tube. Then do the following:

- Choose someone at random from your class.

- Empty your pipette into your contact's test tube as he/she does the same to you.

- Place the stopper in your test tube and shake your test tube gently to mix solutions.

- In the data table (Round 1) write down the name of the person with whom you exchanged solutions.

Repeat Step 2 twice more (Rounds 2 and 3), each time with a different contact.

When you have exchanged solutions with three different contacts, add one drop of phenol red to your test tube to see if you are infected with the "disease." Two test results are possible:

Solution turns red!! — You have the disease!

Solution turn yellow — You are not infected. (Whew!)

Complete the class data table below using information from

Figure 25. Students Work Together to Discover the Source of a Disease.

> **ACTIVITY 3-8**
>
> - In small groups, create a storyboard for a commercial advertising an imaginary soap product. Develop your commercial as you wish, but you must include the formation of micelles as part of your sales pitch.
> - Share your storyboard with the rest of the class.
>   Remember: Your drawings for the storyboard do not have to be highly developed. They should be diagrams. You can use stick figures and other simplified forms to get your idea across clearly.

Figure 26. Students Communicate to Each Other Ideas About Chemistry.

> *Situation:* You need to run a temporary cold-water pipe from the nearest water fountain to the wall behind your teacher's desk. The pipe should run along the floor next to the wall and through the doorway. Determine how many 10-foot sections of $\frac{3}{4}$-inch pipe, how many $\frac{3}{4}$-inch unions (straight pipe to join sections), and how many $\frac{3}{4}$-inch 90° elbows (curved pipe for the turns) are needed. Determine how much the material for the cold-water pipe will cost.
>
> **a.** Based on this situation, write instructions to your classmate describing what you want done.
>
> **b.** **1.** Exchange instructions with your classmate and carry out the instructions you receive. Do exactly what the instructions say, even if you think they are wrong.
>
> **2.** Determine how much pipe material you need and what it will cost.
>
> With your classmate, discuss the results you got by following the

Figure 27. Students Work Together to Learn How to Read and Write Technical Instructions.

Students also must cooperate to complete the many small-group activities that are included in the applied academics courses. For example, one Applied Biology/Chemistry activity instructs students to work as a simulated commercial advertising team. Their assignment is to create a "storyboard" for a soap commercial that explains how soap dissolves grease. (It does this through the formation of micelles, particles that are negatively charged at one end and nonpolar at the other.) In order to carry out this activity, each student will have to understand the mechanism by which micelles do their work. In addition, the group will have to cooperate to develop a plot for the commercial, to invent a consistent style for the diagrams in the storyboard, and agree on a fair distribution of work in the execution of the board and the sales pitch.

Partnering can be a particularly effective strategy for encouraging students to cooperate. The previously mentioned math problem in which two students are required to write instructions for one another is a good example. This exercise requires each student, acting as the other student's employee, to do exactly what the instructions say "even if you think they are wrong." Later the results of this activity are discussed by the two students. Each one, in effect, provides feedback to his or her "employer" concerning the accuracy and clarity of the instructions. Then the students have the opportunity to rewrite the instructions to make them as clear as possible. Only at this point does the teacher review the written materials.

Are Applied Academics Working?

Because even the oldest applied-academics curricula are still relative newcomers in the classroom,[8] significant data regarding the success of these efforts are only now beginning to accrue. Since about 1990, however, several independent studies have tracked the success of applied academics through various measures of student performance. The results of these studies have been both significant and encouraging. In addition, anecdotal evidence from teachers and students and the results of informal studies and surveys reveal high levels of success for applied-academics curricula.

It is important to understand, however, that student performance is only one factor to consider in determining the success of applied academics. If we are truly looking for different approaches to teaching and learning, our expectations and assessments should reflect these differences.

What should our expectations for success be? I, along with many of my colleagues—especially Leno Pedrotti, the principal designer of several of the applied-academics courses—would consider an applied-academics curriculum to be a success if the following criteria apply:

- Students are able to transfer knowledge from academic content to vocational applications and from school to the workplace.

- Students are not afraid to take academic subjects such as math and science.

- Students display more interest, motivation, and understanding of the value of the subject and of school in general than they did in classes taught by traditional methods.

---

8. Principles of Technology was piloted in 1984, Applied Economics in 1983, Applied Mathematics and Applied Communication in 1987–88. Applied Biology/Chemistry was still undergoing a pilot phase in 1993.

- The applied course is as challenging as the traditional "college-prep" course on the same subject—not low-level or watered-down.

- The student population that has traditionally done poorly in academic subjects displays improved performance.

- Applied courses receive the same recognition/acceptance from universities and colleges as do the traditional courses with the same content.

The evidence of student accomplishment that I will share is significant and supportive of these expectations.

Because applied academics are different from most teaching resources and curricula, a different set of assumptions has been tied to the evaluation of these curricula. To evaluate the success of the applied programs accurately, the majority of the consultants, teachers, educators, and curriculum designers who played a role in the development and/or evaluation of applied academics have made the following assumptions about those who would be teaching and learning in these courses:

- Most of the students enrolled in an applied-academics course traditionally have not been high achievers in that subject or discipline.

- Most of the students enrolled in applied-academics courses do not have significant learning disabilities.

- Most of the teachers of the applied-academics curricula are certified in the academic subject/discipline in which they teach.

- Teachers have not necessarily used the pedagogy of applied/ contextual methodology in the teaching of their courses in the past.

- All teachers of applied-academics courses have received training in the different teaching methods, lab equipment, and the overall management of materials and activities related to the academic course in question.

With these expectations and assumptions in mind, I will review some of the independent studies on applied academics—studies that demonstrate clearly that applied academics have met or even exceeded our goals for students.

All of the studies vary in the numbers, ages, and abilities of students, as well as the curricula that were evaluated. However, each study fits in at least one of the following categories: content assessment, teacher/student response, and university acceptance.

Evaluating the Success of Applied Mathematics

A Math Teachers' Study (Content Assessment, Teacher/Student Response)

In 1991–93 a comparison of Algebra I completers with Applied Mathematics II completers was conducted based on an algebra test written by mathematics teachers and reviewed by five state math supervisors and consultants. The test was administered to more than eight hundred Algebra I students and over three hundred Applied Mathematics II students spread across twenty-four high schools in sixteen states.[9] Its purpose was to determine whether the students completing Applied Mathematics II were ready for entry into Algebra II. This assessment was a follow-up to the same study conducted in 1991–92.

Students represented inner-city, urban, suburban, and rural settings and grade levels from ninth to twelfth grades. In addition, all students in the Applied Mathematics course represented the lower 70 percent of the student body in terms of academic achievement.

An analysis of the test results indicates that the two-year sequence of Applied Mathematics does indeed enable completers to develop algebra skills comparable to or exceeding those of students completing a first-year algebra course. This is evidenced by the fact that the Applied Mathematics II students (see figures 24 and 25):

- had average scores comparable to those of Algebra I students. (The low average scores—in the middle 40 percent for either group area—indicate the overall difficulty of the exam.)

- compared well with Algebra I completers on a majority of the thirty-six test items.

- compared well with Algebra I completers on a majority of the algebra competencies measured.

These results also imply that Applied Mathematics students have lowered their anxiety levels about math and have developed the background necessary to take higher-level courses in mathematics. In addition, the Applied Mathematics students have developed a sense for how their mathematical skills apply to various occupational areas—a sense that completers of the traditional algebra course may not have.

---

9. The disparity in the base numbers is due to an early decision to disqualify all students who claimed to have "had some algebra" before. This decision was made to ensure the overall quality of results.

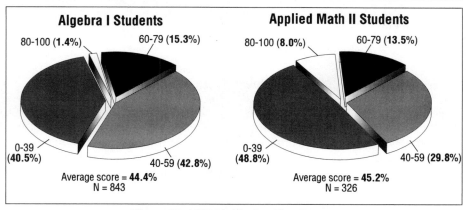

Figure 28. 1992-93 Algebra Test Scores

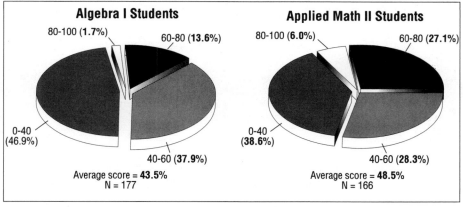

Figure 29. 1991-92 Algebra Test Scores

A Report from the University of Georgia (University Acceptance)

In a 1993 report to the Georgia Department of Education, members of the Science Education Department of the University of Georgia verified that, with properly certified instructors, Applied Math I and II are equivalent to Algebra I and should be shown as such on the high school transcript.

The study done by the Science Education Department shows significant improvement of test grades of students who had not done well in previous math courses. The study indicates that:

Thirteen of the eighteen teachers reported a very high rate of student success, grades of B and A, in Applied Mathematics. They attribute this success, with students who had not previously been successful in mathematics, to the positive attitudes students had toward the material and the activity oriented approach to teaching as opposed to direct instruction and practice. Twelve of the eighteen teachers cited the relevance of the curriculum as a factor in engendering positive student attitudes.[10]

An Applied Mathematics Class in Oklahoma (Teacher/Student Response)

As a math teacher at Pawhuska High School in Pawhuska, Oklahoma, Linda Graham feels that the best demonstration of success in Applied Mathematics was the testimonials she received from her students. Following are some student responses she collected after two weeks of class. (Student names have been omitted by request from the teacher.) While far from a scientific sampling, they do represent the overall tone of the students' response to the Applied Mathematics course.

I knew Applied Math wouldn't be easy for me. Math never is. I'm learning how to comprehend problems and think them through instead of just doing the mechanics of math. I like being able to have a group or partner.

At first I was kind of embarrassed to be in Applied Math. I felt like I wasn't very smart. After the class started, I got really excited about it. I feel like I'm learning.

At first I thought this would be boring, dull, and basically a waste of time, but now I think this class is going to be challenging and really a big help to my math skills! I've never been good with story problems but so far this class seems to be making it easier for me to understand!

The first time I heard about Applied Math I didn't know what to think, but now I realize that it isn't a "dummy course." I think it will benefit us all.

Applied Math has helped me out a lot this year. I have learned more in this class than I have in any other math class I've been in. I am comfortable working with my classmates in groups and asking questions, as before, I was very shy and afraid to ask questions.

Evaluating the Success of Applied Economics

An Independent Comparison (Content Assessment)

In 1992-93, a firm called Formative Evaluation Research Associates conducted a study of the Applied Economics curriculum that has been developed, tested, and implemented through Junior Achievement, Inc. For the study, students in twenty Applied Economics classes from across the country were matched with similar students in traditional economics classes.

---

10. Bill McKillip, Ed Davis, Tom Koballa, and Steve Oliver, *A Study of Applied Math and Principles of Technology Relative to the College Prep Curriculum*, a report for the Department of Education of Georgia (Atlanta, GA: University of Georgia Science Education Department, July 1992), 19.

Each student took the Test of Economic Literacy (TEL), a respected, nationally normed test of economic knowledge geared to high school students.

After both groups had taken both the pre-tests and post-tests of the TEL, researchers found that the Applied Economics students had outperformed the other students on the post-test by a statistically significant margin. Not only did the Applied Economics students score higher on thirty-six of the forty-six TEL items; they also scored higher on each general subject area—Fundamental Economic Concepts, Microeconomics, Macroeconomics, and International Economics.

Evaluating the Success of Principles of Technology (Applied Physics)

A Field Test at Iowa State (Content Assessment)

In 1989, Iowa State University conducted a similar field test, comparing students who had completed traditional physics classes with those who had completed Principles of Technology. The study involved 675 high school students in fifteen Iowa districts. The final report details these results:

> All students took a pre-test to determine their physics knowledge before starting the physics [traditional] or PT (Principles of Technology) courses. As expected, the physics students outscored the industrial education students by an average of five points. The test was re-administered after one year of physics and PT instruction, and the results were considerably different. PT students not only made up the initial five-point differential, but they outscored the physics students by an average of 11 points, a total swing of 17 points. The physics students gained 12 points while the PT students gained 29 points.[11]

An Evaluation at a Nebraska High School

In 1991–93, Papillion LaVista High School in Papillion, Nebraska administered the Armed Services Vocational Aptitude Battery Test (ASVAB) to students enrolled in both traditional physics courses and the Principles of Technology course. Both pre-tests and post-tests were administered in an effort to compare the achievement of the two groups. It is important to note, however, that the achievement levels of the two groups *before* taking the courses were quite disparate. Approximately 33 percent of the physics students were in the top 10 percent of their class and 90 percent of them were in the top 50 percent of their class. By contrast, about 94 percent of the Principles of Technology students were in the bottom 50 percent of their class.

---

11. John Dugger, "Principles of Technology Versus High School Physics: A Comparison of Student Achievement," a presentation to the International Technology Education Association Conference, Dallas, TX, March 1989.

The tests showed that the average growth for the Principles of Technology student was 38.1 percent, while the average growth for the physic students was 33.6. These results led the teachers at this school to conclude that students who are traditionally poor achievers can be motivated and interested in their curriculum if it is taught in an applied/contextual manner.[12]

An Auburn University Study (Content Assessment)

A report by Richard Baker, James Noel Wilmoth, and Bert Lewis of the Center for Vocational and Adult Education, Auburn University, summarizes the results of a case study conducted by the Center to compare the performance of students enrolled in high school Principles of Technology courses with those enrolled in traditional physics. A total of 226 Principles of Technology students and 306 physics students were randomly selected throughout Alabama to participate in the test, which was extracted from a nationally recognized high school physics exam and encompassed the areas of mechanics, heat, and electricity.

The resulting data were analyzed according to three student groupings determined on the basis of performance on the SAT math test: lower-quartile students in one group, second- and third-quartile students in a middle group, and upper-quartile students in a third group. The researchers concluded that "Principles of Technology is a sound course, equivalent to physics, in terms of student performance on a test of physics items."

Furthermore the researchers recommended that "counselors should not hesitate to encourage *both college-bound students* (both 2 and 4 year) *and students who will upon high school graduation immediately enter the engineering-related technology/mechanical workforce* to enroll in Principles of Technology."[13]

One Teacher's Study in Tennessee (Teacher/Student Response)

While the authors of Principles of Technology never intended for it to replace the traditional physics course, it does teach many similar concepts. And because it improves student confidence and motivation, it also serves as a launching pad into the sciences for students who otherwise would have steered clear of such "hard" courses.

Patsy River, a physics teacher at Hickman County High School in Centerville, Tennessee, first noticed this tendency by observing the

---

12. Outcomes provided through informal study conducted by Joanne Langabee, Physics Teacher, Papillion LaVista High School by letter to Leno Pedrotti, Senior Vice President, Center for Occupational Research and Development.

13. Richard Baker, James Noel Wilmoth, and Bert Lewis, *Factors Affecting Student Achievement in a High School Principles of Technology Course: A Case Study*, a report for the Center for Vocational and Adult Education (Auburn, AL: Auburn University, 1989).

enrollment in her regular physics class after Principles of Technology had been implemented in her high school. In 1989, one year after Principles of Technology was first offered, Patsy became aware that two students out of her seven-student class had previously taken Principles of Technology. As she continued to monitor the enrollment in her physics classes over the next three years, she discovered the following:

- In 1990–91, three out of fourteen physics students (21 percent) had taken Principles of Technology.

- In 1991–92, nine out seventeen physics students (53 percent) had taken Principles of Technology.

- In 1991–93, twelve out of thirty-one physics students (39 percent) had taken Principles of Technology.

Patsy River's informal study would seem to indicate that students who would not normally enroll in physics had taken the Principles of Technology course, built up their confidence and appreciation for science, and decided to continue building their academic knowledge by electing to take the traditional physics course. Patsy is convinced that Principles of Technology has opened the minds of many of her students who otherwise would have lacked the confidence to try a college-prep course and has therefore opened doors for them to be mainstreamed back into more traditional science offerings.

Evaluating the Success of Combined Applied-Academics Curricula

An SREB Field Study

In 1992, the Southern Regional Education Board published some of the first field-test data comparing the performance of students who had completed two years of applied-academics courses with those who had taken traditional academics courses. (These data resulted from a study conducted between 1988 and 1990). Consistently, the math and science proficiencies tested by nationally normed assessment measures reflected raised scores and significant accomplishments by completers of the applied-academic courses. Comparative results between pilot sites with a greater number of traditional mathematics students versus sites with a greater number of Applied Mathematics students (see figure 30) indicate that Applied Mathematics students scored as well as or better than students who took the traditional mathematics courses. These results were similar to those found in comparative studies of Principles of Technology and Applied Biology/ Chemistry with traditional science courses.

Percentage of students enrolled in:	SITE A	SITE B
General Math	4%	52%
Pre-Algebra	54%	1%
Algebra I	88%	67%
Algebra II	60%	37%
Geometry	82%	46%
Higher-Level Math	18%	14%
Applied Math	2%	46%
Total Math Credits	3.3	2.6
Completed 2 Upper-Level Math Courses	79%	38%
NAEP Scores	296.8	298.5

Note: The percentages and the credits were derived from an analysis of student transcript information. The math scores represent the achievement of 1990 vocational completers at two sites on National Assessment of Educational Progress math tests. The two sites are comparable in size, school organization, and socioeconomic background of students tested. The difference in scores is statistically significant.

Figure 30. SREB Pilot Site Comparison of Student Achievement in Applied Mathematics Versus Traditional Mathematics Curriculum[14]

A Report from Washington State (Teacher/Student Response)

In 1991–92, the Northwest Regional Educational Laboratory (NWREL) conducted an evaluation of an applied-academics project sponsored by the Boeing Company throughout the state of Washington. NWREL used surveys to evaluate three applied-academics curricula (Principles of Technology, Applied Mathematics, and Applied Communication) being taught in more than thirty high schools across the state. The purpose was to gain insight into how the applied-academics classes operate and fit within the total curriculum.

The survey included 32 teachers of Principles of Technology, 8 teachers of Applied Mathematics, and 16 teachers of Applied Communication. When asked whether they would recommend the curricula to other teachers, most (in some cases all) of the respondents said that they would. All teachers felt that the curriculum had a positive impact on academic achievement, understanding of subject content, and relevance of the subject matter to the world of work. The Principles of Technology teachers agreed that the curriculum promoted academic/vocational integration and that the curriculum could be learned by all students.

The NWREL evaluators also surveyed 653 Principles of Technology students and 137 Applied Mathematics students. More than 80 percent of

---

14. Gene Bottoms, Alice Presson, and Mary Johnson, *Making High Schools Work: Through Integration of Academic and Vocational Education* (Atlanta: Southern Regional Education Board, 1992), 64-65. This table is printed with permission by the Southern Regional Education Board, copyright 1992.

each set of students said they would recommend the course in question to their friends, and nearly 50 percent indicated that the course was better than previous math and science courses they had taken. Students indicated overwhelmingly that the strengths of the applied courses were the hands-on focus, the teamwork emphasis, and the real-life application.

A Vote of University Confidence (University Acceptance)

As indicated earlier, more and more universities nationwide are recognizing the strength of applied-academics courses and giving them a vote of confidence by agreeing to accept them as prerequisites for admission. (The specific type of credit varies with the course and the university.)

During the spring of 1993, for example, the State University System of Florida formally announced that Applied Mathematics I and II as well as Principles of Technology were acceptable for public university admission statewide. This action has led to a commitment to publicize this decision through a series of statewide meetings with high school counselors, the development of a revised counseling manual (Counseling for Postsecondary Education) and an updated student tabloid targeting secondary juniors and seniors (Career and Education Planning Guide).

The same time this decision was made in Florida, the University of Wisconsin system also recognized Principles of Technology and Applied Mathematics I and II as applying toward admission to each of the institutions included in the system. In an effort to support and show commitment to the Tech Prep initiative, the university system will note the new acceptance in their 1993-94 "Introduction" publication.

In a similar decision, the Oregon System of Higher Education recommended in 1992 that Applied Economics and Applied Mathematics be recognized as meeting college-preparatory admission standards for social studies and mathematics.

The State of Washington University System has also recently joined the ranks of those accepting applied-academics courses as prerequisites for admission. After lengthy debate, extensive involvement by the Boeing Company (which has played a large role in sponsoring Tech Prep in the Northwest), and many testimonials from secondary school teachers, the system unanimously accepted the Principles of Technology course as an equivalent to college-preparatory science. (See chapter 7 for more information on the acceptance process.)

There's More to Do

Applied academics have come a long way since the first pilot programs for Principles of Technology. But much more needs to be done in order for

Tech Prep and applied academics to reach their potential as instruments of true educational reform.

For example, more work needs to be done in *devising appropriate ways to evaluate student success* in applied-academics courses. Traditional methods of assessment and evaluation (including those cited in this chapter) often use multiple-choice questions to evaluate students on their ability to solve for the right answer. Such tests require students to use some problem-solving, analytical/computational, and verbal skills, but they do little to evaluate the students' abilities to relate, transfer, apply, experience, and work coopera- tively. And they never even address the question of whether student success should be measured solely on the basis of the ability to arrive at a single correct answer or the knack for taking a multiple-choice test.

Much also remains to be done in the area of *empowering teachers to teach contextually*—equipping them with adequate resources and training and also providing the information they need about contextual learning and about the relationships of the academic curricula to personal, societal, and especially occupational life. We should not continue to expect teachers to do all the work of seeking out real-life applications and relating them to students through a variety of experiences. Instead, they need the help of employers and other community representatives to make the connection with the workplace that will enrich their teaching. They need adequate training and sufficient release time to learn new teaching methods and become familiar with new materials. (All of the research and field tests conducted on applied academics indicate clearly that the success of the curricula depends heavily on adequate teacher training prior to implementation of the curricula.)

There is still work to be done when it comes to *ensuring institutional and structural support* for teaching and learning that is based on contextual methods. There can be no significant and successful change in curriculum unless considerable resources are allotted for training teachers, purchasing laboratory equipment, and acquiring resources to integrate and apply their content.

Finally, if applied-academics curricula are ever to take their place as respectable components of our national education system, more needs to be done in the area of *improving communication* between education practitioners at various levels and *clearing up misconceptions* about applied academics. Despite the evidence that applied-academics courses can provide a solid academic foundation to the majority of students in our schools, the old stigma of "lesser learning" still seems to linger. To dispel that stigma, more dialogue is needed between all members of the educational community.

Significant progress was made on that front in a recent meeting on contextual learning held in Waco, Texas, in June of 1993. At this meeting, a varied group of educators, including several university admissions directors and secondary school administrators from various states, discussed the question of whether universities should accept applied-academics courses as admissions credits. Debate was lively, but the conference participants reached a consensus on two important points: the need for better understanding of applied academics, and the need for more data about the effectiveness of the applied approach in teaching students academic content. After considerable discussion, however, quite a few of the participants professed a new understanding of and a new willingness to support applied academics and Tech Prep at the local level.

As far as I am concerned, that is the real beauty of the applied-academics approach to education. If it is presented properly and considered with an open mind, it's hard to resist. It's hard to argue with a concept and an approach that is already working to open minds and open doors for hundreds of motivated and excited students across the nation.

5.

SOMETHING TO USE

The Shape of the
Tech Prep Curriculum

SOMETHING TO BUILD ON

When I was a practicing electrical engineer, the two things I needed most in my job were a well-equipped laboratory and a competent technician—especially a competent technician. Like most engineers, I was pretty good at conception and design, but I needed a lot of help in construction, testing, troubleshooting, and repair. The only people who could help me with this work were technicians. And the best technician I ever worked with was Reuben Weinmaster.

Reuben could do anything in the lab—and he seemed to always do it right. I could design a new, high-power laser; but I could not build it and make it operate reliably. Reuben could because he would get (or make) the right parts, assemble them efficiently, and fix it or tweak it to make it run the way I had designed it to run. Reuben knew tools and techniques—but he also knew how lasers were supposed to work (i.e. the scientific and mathematical principles behind the technology).

Reuben Weinmaster and I made a great team. I had a unique role and so did he. Neither of us—engineer nor technician—could function effectively without the other, and we respected each other's unique contributions.

Almost every modern industry needs people like Reuben—people who can build, modify, install, maintain, repair, and calibrate modern sophisticated equipment and processes in laboratories, manufacturing plants, energy-generation systems, processing plants, modern buildings, health-care facilities, transportation, and communication systems. To the people who employ them and work with them, capable technicians are worth their weight in gold.

But capable people like Reuben are valued in other fields as well, although they're not always called technicians. They're called nurses, bookkeepers, paralegals, dietitians, elder-care workers, law-enforcement officers, plant operators, physical therapists, and fashion designers. In their particular fields, in addition to using their job-specific skills and knowledge, they work in teams, solve problems, teach others, and exercise leadership. They use computers, serve customers, and control resources, as well as acquiring, evaluating, storing, and interpreting communications.[1]

Are the people I have just described technicians? They are according to my definition. Unfortunately, however, this term has been misused to refer to just about any level of worker. Just as the term *sanitary engineer* is sometimes used as an inflated term for garbage collectors, the word *technician* has been misused to refer to any menial job where someone does something—for instance, "car wash technicians." But in this book and in the Tech Prep/Associate Degree curriculum, a technician is a highly trained, career-oriented professional with a specialization in a particular field and a sufficiently broad education/background to grow in his or her career.

Tech Prep is about the business of preparing such men and women for their work and for their lives. And that kind of practical, solid preparation is the rationale that shapes the Tech Prep/Associate Degree curriculum.

What Is Different About Tech Prep?

In previous chapters I examine the foundation courses for Tech Prep and the learning theory behind those courses. In this chapter I want to back off and look at the larger picture—at the way the individual classes and the educational theories fit together into an overall course of study.

The examination of curriculum in this chapter is of necessity both *descriptive* and *normative*; I am describing both existing Tech Prep curriculum and theoretical models. Because Tech Prep is a relatively new and still evolving initiative, I believe this is a helpful approach. We need to draw on past and current experience, but we also need to work toward what we believe Tech Prep can be.

Before we look at the specific characteristics of the Tech Prep curriculum, however, it might be helpful to review some of the basic qualities that make this particular course of study different from other educational curricula.

---

1. All of these "other" skills are identified as essential to the workplace in the Secretary's Commission on Achieving Necessary Skills, *What Work Requires of Schools: A SCANS Report for America 2000* (Washington, DC: Government Printing Office, 1992).

Tech Prep Is Different from Vocational Education

First of all, Tech Prep is distinctive from vocational education in that it not only trains people to get their first job, but also prepares them for an entire career. In addition, it prepares students for further education and training; that is, they "learn to learn." This requires an early, solid foundation in academic skills—taught in a way that makes it easier for most students to learn, but not watered down or oversimplified.

Because of this academic emphasis, the Tech Prep/Associate Degree curriculum clearly cannot be a patch-up job on existing vocational or technical programs. The entire curriculum structure must change in order first to build, and then to build upon—the strong foundation of applied academics.

Tech Prep Is Different from College Prep

Tech Prep also differs from secondary programs commonly known as college-prep programs. In the literal sense, of course, Tech Prep *is* college prep; it prepares a student to earn an associate's degree at a community or technical college. But what is generally referred to as college prep is a high school program of studies that prepares students to pursue a baccalaureate degree, or higher, at a four-year college or university.

Tech Prep differs from this form of college prep in three ways:

1. Tech Prep requires the same standards of academic accomplishment as college prep, but it teaches content through courses based on contextual learning methods (applied academics).

2. Tech Prep creates higher interest levels in most students by attaching a career focus to the program of study.

3. Tech Prep prepares students to be competent according to work (employer) standards as well as academic (school) standards.

A Curriculum Whose Time Has Come

As the Tech Prep movement has grown in size and acceptance, its goals and structure have changed significantly, evolving in response to emerging needs, new understandings, and practical experience. If it is to keep on growing and succeeding, it must continue to evolve. In the process, Tech Prep calls for major changes in educational organizations as well as in the attitudes and practices of administrators and teachers. It calls for open minds on the part of all concerned—especially educators—as it seeks to open doors of articulation between educational institutions and doors of opportunity in today's workplace.

Ten years ago, Tech Prep was first introduced as "2+2 articulation"—an occupationally oriented curriculum that tied together (articulated) the last two years of high school and the first two years of postsecondary education at a community college. It was intended to be a vocational alternative to the more academically oriented college-prep curriculum.

Since that time, however, we have come to recognize the ability of all students to master academic concepts through contextual teaching/learning techniques. We also have come to recognize the need for today's workers to master these academic concepts and be able to use them in the workplace. These new understandings, along with the combined experience of the Tech Prep programs that have been put into operation over the past ten years, have caused the basic concept of Tech Prep to evolve toward its current curriculum structure.

Today, Tech Prep/Associate Degree stands at the cutting edge of educational reform. It is a mature and comprehensive approach to education featuring a 4+2 system of articulation (grades nine through fourteen) that begins with applied academics taken in the ninth and tenth grades. Strongly oriented toward helping students achieve the skills and knowledge they will need to compete in today's workplace, Tech Prep calls for an active partnership between secondary schools, postsecondary schools, and business and industry (the future employers of Tech Prep students).

Oriented Toward Outcome

What are the marks of a successful Tech Prep curriculum? First, Tech Prep is doing its job if it achieves the following outcomes:

- Students receive a strong academic foundation in math, science, and communication skills.

- Students are given the opportunity to explore and identify a career interest.

- Students are helped to prepare for a specific career goal.

- Students are connected with a technical/career specialization related to employment specifications.

- Students come to understand the workplace and employers' expectations for workers.

- Students are given the opportunity and ability to pursue further education and training, including (if desired) the baccalaureate degree.

- Students have the chance to participate in educational electives such as the arts, sports, and organizational leadership.

- Students retain the option of changing their academic or career pursuits.

- Students receive sufficient preparation to qualify for employment after high school graduation if they do not enroll immediately in a community college.

Meeting such stated objectives is especially important to the design of a Tech Prep curriculum because Tech Prep is essentially an *outcome-based* program. Student success is measured not by grades but by *competencies;* that is, the student must demonstrate the ability to perform certain measurable tasks.

The specifications or expected outcomes for a Tech Prep curriculum are the competencies required for job performance and career growth within a student's chosen field. For example, a set of competencies for an office worker might include the ability to type; the ability to use word processing, database, and spreadsheet software on office computer systems; the ability to file information efficiently and retrieve it quickly; and the ability to transcribe business correspondence. A similar set of competencies for an engineering technology technician might include the ability to troubleshoot, repair, calibrate, and operate a complex piece of equipment like a telecommunications system, a computer, or a photocopy machine.

Ideally these job competencies should be determined by the standards for employment set by employers and by labor leaders for a given job or group of jobs. And a significant amount of activity at state and federal levels is currently underway to delineate the standards for certain groups of applications.

Unfortunately, however, many of the job groupings being developed at present are being determined according to the businesses they represent; for example, all jobs in the computer industry, including design, repair, operation, and sales would be grouped together. A distinct improvement would be to group occupations according to commonality of knowledge/skills required to do the job; for instance, all occupations requiring a background in electronics might be grouped together, even those that serve different industries. Such a development would dovetail with the cluster emphasis of the Tech Prep curriculum (to be explained later in this chapter) and would enable a smoother transition from school to work.

A Multiphase Curriculum

When the "need to know and do"—the desired, job-based educational outcomes—is established, it is the role of educators at the secondary and postsecondary level to organize the scope and sequence of the academic/technical content and the laboratory/job experiences required to help students achieve these outcomes. It is this overall arrangement of content and experience that comprises the Tech Prep curriculum.

Although an articulated program like Tech Prep will eventually need to be divided into a secondary component, a postsecondary component, and perhaps a worksite component, the total curriculum should ideally be designed and organized as a single sequence, without regard for where or by whom the course work will be taught. When the design is complete, it will become appropriate to sort out which elements will be taught by high schools, which will be taught by community colleges, and which will be taught by employers.

What would a typical Tech Prep curriculum structure look like? Figure 1 outlines a suggested model for a 4+2 curriculum and indicates the components and outcomes for each phase of the Tech Prep program. This model divides the curriculum into three major two-year phases.

The first phase, which begins in the ninth grade, is the *Tech Prep foundation* component. At the beginning of the ninth-grade year, students select the Tech Prep plan (as opposed to the college-prep program). At this early stage,

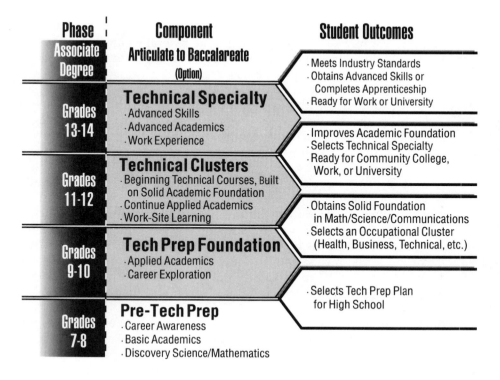

Figure 1. Components and Outcomes for Each Phase of the Tech Prep Curriculum

all Tech Prep students regardless of occupational interest follow a common curriculum, building a foundation through applied-academics courses and career exploration (as well as taking basic courses required for graduation).

Some states already are requiring some form of written plan, often called an education and/or employability development plan, to be drawn up at this age. The plan may specify courses and work experiences in which the students will engage and competencies they will be required to demonstrate. Such plans are intended to be flexible or subject to change so that "tracking" of the students is avoided. At the same time, students are required to commit to a plan to avoid drifting through a series of courses in high school.

At the end of this initial two-year phase, Tech Prep students should be well on their way to obtaining a solid foundation in math, science, and communication skills and should have received the help they need to make an informed decision about what kind of specialty they may want to pursue. Then, as they enter eleventh grade, they are asked to settle on a specific occupational *cluster* (a related group of occupations, such as business, health services, engineering technology occupations, or human services) from which they will later choose a more specific occupation.

Phase two, which encompasses the eleventh and twelfth grades, is the *technical clusters* component of the curriculum. During this phase, in addition to taking more applied-academics courses and general courses required for graduation, students begin to take technical courses that teach skills applicable to a particular group of careers.

Students enrolled in certain fields may also take some specialty courses, which may be combined with worksite learning experiences. For instance, a skills-oriented program such as welding might require that students begin taking actual welding classes in the eleventh and twelfth grades, especially if they plan to go to work immediately after high school graduation. This is also true for programs that are built through "magnet" high schools specializing in certain professions such as health care or criminal justice. Students will leave these magnet high schools with enough specialty courses to qualify for entry-level jobs in these fields.

Phase two of the Tech Prep curriculum ends with graduation from high school. At this point the Tech Prep students should have acquired enough basic technical skills to seek entry-level work in their chosen specialty. Or they may choose at this point to enter a university and work toward a baccalaureate degree. (They should be able to do this with a minimum of additional preparation.)

If they continue with the Tech Prep curriculum, however, the students then will enter the third, or *technical specialty* component. For the next two years, they will be gaining advanced skills and/or work experience in their chosen field of specialization. Ideally, they will be enrolled in an associate degree program at a community college with the possibility of a worksite learning component such as mentoring or apprenticeship.

At the completion of the third phase, which should last no longer than two years (full time), Tech Prep completers will have one or more of three types of certification:

- They will have met business/industry standards for employment in their chosen field.

- They will have obtained an associate degree.

- They will have been accepted for continued education at a university so they can work toward a baccalaureate degree.

Note that figure 1 also shows two additional components. One is a *pre-Tech-Prep* component that prepares students for the choices that will move them into either Tech Prep or college prep. This phase, which ideally should begin in kindergarten, would involve contextual learning and career awareness from an early age, preparing students to move smoothly into Tech Prep when they reach ninth grade.

The other additional component would be an articulation from an associate degree to a four-year college or university with the goal of earning a baccalaureate degree. This should always be an option for Tech Prep students, although it is unlikely that a large proportion of Tech Prep students will end up taking this route.

Very little work has been done so far on incorporating either of these "outside" phases into the primary Tech Prep curriculum. Both will need to be clearly defined and understood before Tech Prep can offer the kind of seamless, flexible educational program that today's students need to prepare for the future.

Three Students—Three Paths to Success

Ted, Janice, and Hector are average eighth-grade students. None of them has an interest in pursuing the "college (baccalaureate) prep" plan available to them at Monzano High School, so their eighth-grade counselor encourages them to sign up for the Tech Prep plan instead.

At this point, only Hector has any idea of what kind of career he wants to pursue. His father is an electrical engineer, and Hector has shown an early interest in electronics; he knows right away that the Tech Prep program in electrical engineering is for him. But Ted and Janice know only that they aren't "college-bound." Janice's family doesn't have the money to send her to college, and her grades are not good enough to earn her a scholarship. Ted has always had problems at school; he is planning to drop out as soon as he is old enough.

All three students begin their Tech Prep curriculum in the ninth grade by taking applied classes in math, biology/chemistry, and physics. In these courses, they discover they can do better at these subjects than they ever dreamed possible. They also have the opportunity to get their hands on some electronics equipment and to get some basic training in micro-computers and computer-aided drafting. And Ted and Janice make another discovery during this period: like Hector, they are interested in electronics. Their counselor and teachers notice their talent and interests and talk with all three students about enrolling in the engineering technology career cluster at the beginning of their junior year.

At that point, the three students' paths begin to diverge. Ted's confidence-building applied-academics classes and his time with the counselor have helped him realize that school could be a useful experience for him and have given him an idea of the kind of career he wants. Instead of dropping out, Ted decides to stay in the Tech Prep program through high school graduation, then go to work at an electronics company. Janice, too, elects to continue with Tech Prep, but she wants to complete the entire four-year program. Several sessions with the counselor have convinced her and her parents that college really isn't out of the question. The tuition at their local technical college is low enough that she can go on to finish her associate degree. Hector, on the other hand, has changed his mind about staying in Tech Prep. His Principles of Technology course "turned him on" to school, and after the tenth grade he decides to switch into the "college-prep" curriculum.

Beginning in eleventh grade, therefore, Hector begins to take more advanced courses in math and science to prepare him for university studies. Janice and Ted continue with the second phase of the Tech Prep program and enter the engineering technology cluster. In addition to more applied math and physics courses, they take electronics, mechanics, engineering graphics, and fluid power. Ted also enters an apprenticeship option, continuing to work and learn twenty hours per week at a local electronics company.

After high school graduation, Hector goes on to the state university, where he follows in his father's footsteps to become an electrical engineer. Ted goes to work full time with the electronics company that supported his apprenticeship program. He likely will take advanced courses after hours at the community college after he has completed his apprenticeship training. And Janice continues her electronics study full time at the community college, specializing in telecommunications. After two more years she receives her associate degree in that field and takes a job as a field service technician at MCI Communications. She also applies to the engineering technology program at the local state university. She plans to study part time until she earns her bachelor's degree.

A Common Core and Career Clusters

Another important aspect of the Tech Prep curriculum is that it is designed around the concept of "core skills"—basic skills that are applicable to any of a group of specialties. This foundational concept expresses itself, as we have seen, in career clusters, groups of occupations that share the need for certain basic competencies.

I first became aware of the possibilities of structuring curricula around career clusters in the late seventies, when I was involved in developing a postsecondary engineering curriculum. As we examined various existing curricula, we recognized the many similarities between ten to twelve different engineering technology curricula in electromechanical specialty areas such as electronics, telecommunications, computers, laser/electro-optics, instrumentation/control, and automated manufacturing. Technicians working in the various engineering technologies were all required to

- use basic principles, concepts, and laws of physics and technology in practical applications;

- use algebra, trigonometry, and analytic geometry as problem-solving tools (An understanding of higher mathematics—including computer language and some calculus—may be required.);

- analyze, troubleshoot and repair systems composed of subsystems in three or more of the following areas: electronic, electrical, mechanical, thermal, hydraulic/pneumatic, and optical;

- use materials, processes, apparatuses, procedures, equipment, methods, and techniques common to most technological procedures;

- apply detailed knowledge in one field of specialization with an understanding of the applications and industrial processes in that field;

- use computers for information management, equipment and process control, and design; and

- record, analyze, interpret, synthesize, and transmit facts and ideas with objectivity—and communicate information effectively by oral, written, and graphical means.

By reorganizing each of the engineering technology curricula to identify common course competencies, we were able to come up with a common core of skills and knowledge that could support a cluster of different but related occupations. All of the engineering technology specialty curricula, for instance, could be based on a common core of basic academic skills plus the basic skills listed above.

The strength and flexibility of such an approach soon became apparent. Another set of engineering technology curriculum specialties (for instance, hazardous materials/waste management, biotechnology, laboratory science, or environmental technology) could be constructed using a biology/ chemistry core. And similar core curriculum structures could be designed for health occupations, human services, business/marketing, agriculture/ agribusiness, or other groups of careers.

This common-core, career-cluster approach has proved eminently adaptable and appropriate for Tech Prep/Associate Degree initiatives. Figure 2 depicts how it might work in a typical Tech Prep program. (These particular five clusters have been chosen arbitrarily. Other groupings of occupational clusters are possible and may be preferable, depending on the needs of the community.)

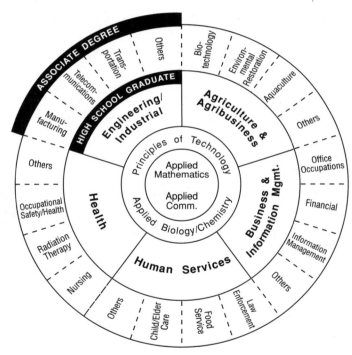

Figure 2. The Core of a TPAD Curriculum

The center of the diagram depicts the beginning point for the curriculum; all students would begin at this "core" and work their way "outward," acquiring increasingly specialized knowledge and skills.

In the first two years (ninth and tenth grades), the curriculum emphasis is on using applied-academics courses to build a foundation of academic competencies that will be used in later, more specialized courses. At the beginning of the eleventh grade, the student chooses one of the five occupational clusters and begins taking technical courses that are basic to that cluster (but applicable to any of the particular careers in the cluster). Upon high school graduation, the student will enter even more specialized training through work experience, advanced-skills courses at a community college, or both.

The career-cluster approach to curriculum design is based on the idea that a variety of different occupations/jobs require similar basic skills. It is also based on the belief that certain basic skills and knowledge are essential for all students, regardless of the profession to which they aspire. It makes sense, therefore, for a student to begin by learning these basic, common skills; move on to acquire the basic skills necessary for a given group of jobs; then learn the specific applications for a specific job.

The essential basic skills and technical core together comprise approximately 80 percent of the overall Tech Prep curriculum. Specific specialty courses, usually taken during the last phase of the Tech Prep program, are the only ones that are unique to a technical or vocational program option. Figure 3 illustrates how basic skills courses (taken by all students) and the technical core courses (taken by all students within a career cluster) form a foundation for the specialties.

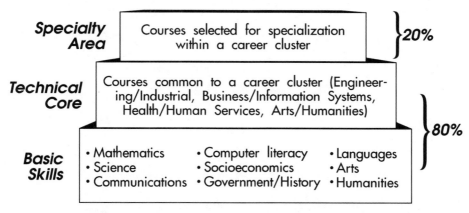

Figure 3. Foundation for Specialties Based on Basic Skills and Technical Core Courses

The career-cluster approach provides school systems with the opportunity to involve larger numbers of students in technical classes and to build a stronger and broader base for the specialty area. This broad base also makes it possible for individuals to change specialties in the future as job opportunities and/or requirements change.

The cluster concept can also link Tech Prep options with traditional college-preparatory options. In other words, some of the basic core material in the clusters can apply to individuals pursuing a baccalaureate degree directly from high school as well as those who aspire to an associate degree or who plan to go directly to employment at the end of high school.

An example of how clustering can serve as an umbrella for selected career options is shown in figure 4. In the diagram, The engineering/industrial cluster includes the engineering, industrial, agricultural, automotive, and construction-related programs. The basic math skills required in these areas are common to all; the requirements for communications and interpersonal skills are very similar; and much of the technology in these fields shares a common basis in applied physics. All of the areas involve machinery and devices and draw heavily upon electrical principles, hydraulic and pneumatic principles, and knowledge of mechanical devices and thermal and optical systems.

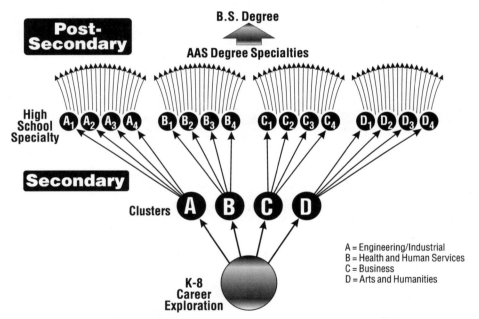

Figure 4. Relationship of Four Career Clusters to Their Related Specialties

The business/information systems cluster includes such occupations as secretarial services, data processing, business management, accounting, and other areas related to the management of enterprises and the processing of information. The advanced math skills required in this area differ somewhat from other clusters, particularly because they involve working with information analysis and processing. An understanding of group behavior, team processes, and organizational dynamics focusing on human behavior is also required.

The health/human services cluster includes such areas of work as health careers, social services, and food and hospitality services. This career cluster is unique in its heavy dependence upon principles of chemistry and the life sciences such as biology and anatomy. The cluster contains a common need for specialized and enhanced interpersonal skills in order to deal with human beings who are in stressful circumstances that threaten their health and well-being.

The arts and humanities cluster rounds out the universe of possible occupational areas. The focus in this cluster is on occupations in the areas of journalism, performing arts, graphic arts, political science, and public services. Meeting the common needs in this cluster requires less depth in specialized mathematics, technology, and sciences than in the other clusters, but much broader exposure to creative, humanistic, and societal concerns.

A Unified Education: Toward a More Integrated Curriculum[2]

The term *integration* has come into common usage as a focus of curriculum reform over the last ten years. Depending on the context, the term has been applied in several ways, often with either a vague or a very narrow definition. However, the guiding principles of Tech Prep and our emerging knowledge about learning processes argue for a more comprehensive view of integration—and a curriculum that places high value on this important educational component.

The word *integration* derives from a Latin term meaning "to complete" or "to make whole," and it is defined and explained by such synonyms as *uniting* or *unifying*. Its most common use in terms of curriculum has been to describe a "horizontal" bridging across academic and vocational areas of curriculum to provide students with exposure to both. Less frequently, the term has been applied to "vertical" linkages between secondary and post-secondary programs—but here the term *articulation* is more commonly used. (Actually, *integration* is a far more encompassing term than *articulation*, which simply means forming a connection between two units without necessarily making changes in either.) Other forms of curriculum linking such as team teaching or writing across the curriculum are often associated with the term *integration*.

Concepts such as contextual learning, experiential learning, and cooperative learning, however, suggest a broader and more comprehensive use of curriculum integration. As we have seen, current educational systems have been criticized because they tend to fragment knowledge and ignore relationships between various course areas as they now exist.

2. Material in this section was excerpted from Walter Edling, "Integration Is More Than We Anticipate," unpublished paper prepared for the Center for Occupational Research and Development, 1993.

Research cited in chapter 3 points to fallacious expectations that most students will be able to assemble these bits and pieces of knowledge to solve real-world challenges. While some students may be successful in this synthesis, the majority are not comfortable or successful learning in fragmented elements. To address this reality and thus facilitate learning for the majority of students, therefore, integration should go beyond superficial linkages or sharing of topics among disciplines.

In curriculum design, integration involves two dimensions: horizontal or concurrent relationships and vertical or sequential relationships. There is nothing new about these dimensions; they have long been recognized in curriculum designs. However, traditional integration efforts have not progressed very far beyond definitions of corequisites (concepts that need to be learned simultaneously) and prerequisites (concepts that must be learned in a certain order).

What is newly emerging is the understanding of the critical importance of *comprehensive integration* and its beneficial impact upon students. Educators are beginning to recognize the benefits of a curriculum that

- smoothly combines academic subjects with their real-life applications,

- helps students make connections between traditionally separate disciplines such as math and science, biology and chemistry, science and communications), and

- maps out a seamless program of learning that progresses smoothly from phase to phase without regard to institution.

The applied-academics materials described in chapter 4 represent the first major successful effort to build improved integration into the curriculum design at the secondary level. The success and acceptance of these materials attest to the value of integrating practical, work-related applications into academic course materials while retaining the integrity of the academic content. Other emerging projects are pursuing similar or related integration goals. These include Project 2061, which seeks to integrate the disciplines of science; the integrated math program supported by the National Science Foundation; and the Seattle, Washington, applied-academics project that is developing course materials in applied humanities (see chapter 4).

Unfortunately, integrated approaches to education have so far failed to establish a significant toehold at the postsecondary level. The original applied-academics material (a course called Unified Technical Concepts, see chapter 7) was developed as a postsecondary course prior to the development of the secondary version, but its usage has been limited, and other models have failed to achieve wide acceptance. Until more community and technical colleges open their minds to the benefits of the integrated approach, the goal of seamless vertical integration for Tech Prep programs will not be fully realized.

A Model Integrated Curriculum Structure

To reach its full and effective potential, the Tech Prep program requires a *completely new* curriculum. It must be viewed as the equivalent of a six-year educational experience that begins in the ninth grade and continues through two years of postsecondary education. This seamless, integrated curriculum must combine academic and vocational content as well as classroom, laboratory, and worksite environments, and it must smoothly move a student from a broad foundational education into eventual specialization and preparation for careers.

Logically, the curriculum design requires active input and participation from secondary, postsecondary, and workplace representatives. Such cooperation typically results in elimination of courses that are duplicated at the secondary and postsecondary levels, less remediation at the postsecondary level, and more emphasis on achieving more advanced skills for entering the workplace.

What would a fully integrated Tech Prep curriculum look like? A model of such a curriculum is presented in figure 5. It is important to note several elements that are conspicuously (and deliberately) absent from the model. For example, no "course" structures are shown, nor are there expressions of specific discipline areas such as math, English, or social studies. I believe these traditional structures are the greatest hurdle to overcome in redesigning curriculum with a view toward integration; it's easy to get stuck in the old, fragmented views of learning. Packaging or structure can always be provided later in the design process, but should not be a historical constraint at the outset.

Note also that the terms *vocational* and *academic* are not used; rather the concepts of core and specialized skills are identified to distinguish between areas of *general* utility to all students (basic skills) and areas *specific* to fields of endeavor (specialized application skills).

Basic skills includes topics from areas now known as vocational as well as academic (for example team skills, understanding of systems, critical thinking, or employability skills). Specialized applications skills would include the application of math, science, economics, political science, or communications to specific occupational areas as well as vocational competencies in those areas. Essentially, the core of basic skills is applicable to all students, the core of technical and application skills contains skills applicable to a cluster or broadly related group of jobs, and the specialized skills are focused on a single job or a very closely related group of jobs.

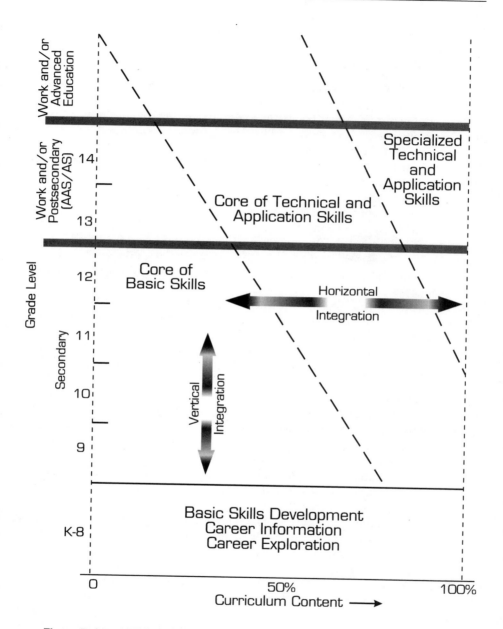

Figure 5. Integration of Basic, Technical, and Specialized Skills in a Tech Prep Curriculum

This model is not specific to any job or even group of jobs. In fact, with only slightly broader interpretation, it would be equally appropriate for a college-preparatory curriculum. In essence, the model diagrams the extent to which individual curricula begin to diverge as every student, Tech Prep or college prep, begins to move toward individual roles in work and life.

Having made those basic observations, let's examine the model more closely. The primary and middle grades (through the eighth grade) focus on development of *basic skills* and knowledge—reading, writing, cultural literacy, computer usage, arithmetic, teamwork, and so on—much as is now the case. What is new in this model is an added emphasis on career information and exploration in these early grades. This dimension would be integrated throughout existing elementary curricula. The purpose is to provide younger students with much more information about the world of work without requiring choices or decisions.

As the student enters the ninth grade, basic skills development continues, but students also begin thinking about a future career and making appropriate curriculum choices that are geared toward career preparation. At this point they also begin the process of acquiring a *core of technical and applications skills*. This process will continue throughout the educational and work life of the student.

Note that this core of technical and application skills is not job-specific; it includes skills that may relate to a range of jobs. Areas of study such as business management, basic electronics, or workplace communications fit in this general category.

Beginning at the eleventh grade, the process of acquiring *career-specific skills* begins. (This process, too, will continue throughout the student's educational and professional life.) This category includes job-specific occupational competencies associated with high school vocational programs as well as technical and professional skills developed at the associate, baccalaureate, and advanced degree levels. It is at this point that nurses learn to manage patient care, bookkeepers learn to use bookkeeping software, and engineering technicians like Reuben learn to do the construction, testing, troubleshooting, and repair that make them so valuable to engineers like me.

A Curriculum That Works

In this chapter, I have tried to lay down some basic guidelines for a successful Tech Prep curriculum. However, the more I understand about Tech Prep curricula, the less prescriptive I want to be. Several years ago, I was prepared to specify a step-by-step process and a specific model for various curricula. Today, after looking at many successful (and many unsuccessful) Tech Prep curricula, I am much less inclined to say that only one way will work. Many current Tech Prep programs are thriving—and will continue to thrive—using significantly different curricula.

Nevertheless, I believe that any successful Tech Prep curriculum will display certain basic characteristics. They have been described in this chapter, and they are more thoroughly developed in the next part of this book. At this point, then, I will simply outline them:

- Tech Prep is a 4+2 curriculum structured on the premise of "build a foundation, build on a foundation,"

- The Tech Prep curriculum is outcome-oriented, geared to providing the higher-order skills required of an advanced workforce.

- Nine basic elements must be present if the curriculum is to deliver the kind of education that today's students need. They are listed on pages 101–102.

- A three-phase curriculum structure builds in maximum effectiveness and flexibility.

- A career-cluster curriculum in the eleventh and twelfth grades enables students to build a broad technical base that can apply to a number of specific careers.

- Academic and technical content should be integrated in specific courses and into the curriculum as a whole.

If all these elements are present, the resulting curriculum should be both solid and flexible, and it should serve a variety of useful purposes to the various people and institutions who are involved in the Tech Prep program.

For the employers of future Tech Prep graduates, for example, the curriculum is an assurance of quality in their future workforce. For counselors and parents, it is a sensible plan that shows students where they are going and how they can become what they want to be. For administrators of the Tech Prep institutions, it is a pact that identifies where, by whom, and to what standards the instruction will be delivered and also describes the resources that will be needed to deliver this instruction. For the Tech Prep teachers, the curriculum is a tool that they have helped design—one that helps them do their job of facilitating student learning.

Most important, the Tech Prep/Associate Degree curriculum is a promise to students that their years in school won't be wasted time, that their education will truly equip them for lifelong work and lifelong learning. In the words of one young student, it gives you "something you can use, something you can build on." In so doing, it is truly an education reform whose time has come.

PART TWO

Making Tech Prep Work

6

TRANS-FORMING

Issues and Answers for Secondary Schools

OUR HIGH SCHOOLS

Forty years ago, the movie *Blackboard Jungle* shocked the nation with its depiction of urban high schools turned into teenage battlegrounds. Today, the scenes of adolescent drug trafficking, teenage pregnancy, and disrespect for authority in any form seem almost as familiar as the evening news. Over the last twenty years, many American high schools seem to have lost their focus to educate and prepare students for life and work. Sometimes it seems as if the major goal for high school students (and teachers) is just to survive!

But in many other high schools across the nation, the tide is beginning to turn. The career focus of a Tech Prep education and the clear relevance of applied academics are opening students' minds and bringing them back into the laboratories and the classrooms. Students are seeing a reason for being in school; teachers and counselors are enjoying their jobs and experiencing a new sense of meaning in their profession. Of course, these changes involve more than just curriculum, but Tech Prep has created more student interest and enthusiasm than most teachers have witnessed in a long time. For this reason, more and more schools are climbing aboard the Tech Prep bandwagon.

Such a transformation, however, is not always easy or painless. Developing a Tech Prep curriculum is a huge task that requires significant effort and adjustment on the part of students, teachers, administrators, parents, school boards, and future employers. Some, for a variety of reasons, will inevitably oppose the changes that are required. Nevertheless, up to this time, the Tech Prep/Associate Degree initiative has made its biggest impact at the high school level. This impact in turn should effect change at other levels of education—before and after high school.

Because Tech Prep has been—and will continue to be—so successful in changing America's high schools, it seems appropriate to begin an exploration of the Tech Prep issues and challenges with a look at the questions and concerns often encountered at the secondary level.

Issue #1: Raising Expectations for the Majority of Students

Consider the number of children you know through family, friends, or other associations who are considered "low-achieving" students. Are these young people often labeled as slow, low-level, or even "dumb"? How many of these students decided early in their educational experience that they were never going to do as well as the top-quartile student? Some of them may have asked you, "Why should I even try?" Almost from the start, they were saddled with a set of low expectations that drained their confidence and sabotaged their chances for success.

Whether by deliberate or unconscious acts, we have classified children as high or low achievers while they are still in the early years of elementary education. And our expectations for them have followed suit. By teaching down to the "low achievers," we have conveyed the message that they just can't handle regular academic subjects. When these students reach high school, they are typically enrolled in watered-down courses in order to just get through school. The students quickly become classified—and classify themselves—as losers.

Should education be a competitive game or sport that generates winners and losers? Clearly no, but that's the way the system is often set up in our secondary schools. Current standards for excellence recognize only a small segment of the high school population—the 25 percent of students who are clearly baccalaureate-bound. These students are the winners. The losers, as any high school student can tell you, are the students who do not perform well in traditional academic courses, who are usually placed in the lower-level curriculum, and who are typically written off very early as not having the potential for higher education.

These students have low expectations for themselves. They lack confidence in how they are perceived by others. In today's workplace, their chances of finding challenging work that supports a decent standard of living are steadily shrinking. And these students comprise half of the high school population!

It may seem obvious to state that we need to hold out higher expectations for more students in more schools. But that is exactly what needs to happen, and it needs to happen at the systemic level. Most educators, employers, and parents are aware of the average U.S. student's dismal performance in math and science as compared to students in other countries. But instead of just calling for higher test scores, I believe we need to address the basic assumptions and methods that underlie the poor achievement—the hierarchy of school subjects, the narrow teaching methodology, and above all, the belief that only a small percentage of students will be able to achieve at high levels.

High expectations for all students mean making room for more than one kind of success in education, doing away with a one-education-fits-all approach, and generating an instructional delivery system that recognizes the differences in interests and learning styles among students. High expectations also mean assuming that all students can learn, retain, and use higher levels of academics than they are achieving now—and then putting a system in place that facilitates this kind of learning. Eliminating watered-down courses, using contextual teaching methods, and focusing education on meaningful outcomes such as careers and higher learning are all effective ways of raising expectations and encouraging students to succeed.

In a number of school systems across the nation, Tech Prep has proved the ideal vehicle for raising expectations—and therefore achievement levels—for secondary students. The teachers and administrators require more of the average students in terms of higher academic achievement in math, science, English, and other areas of basic skills and knowledge. Guidance counselors expect students to start thinking about their future and making choices about their future career. Both parents and faculty expect the students to consider higher education before they consider dropping out. Finally, employers expect to hire an employee with the skills, knowledge, and flexibility to accomplish a wider range of tasks. And in the process, of course, the students' own expectations are raised. Students who once could look forward only to years of low achievement leading to dead-end jobs can now expect to perform well in a curriculum leading to meaningful, well-paid work.

An example of a Tech Prep initiative that emphasizes high expectations would be the Tech Prep program of Swansea High School, the only high school of Lexington School District Four in Swansea, South Carolina. At the time the Tech Prep consortium formed, the school district had the highest dropout rate (7.7 percent) in the state of South Carolina. Only 35 percent of the students continued their education after high school, and their performance on standardized college-entry tests was very low. As a result, the district decided to start the Tech Prep initiative with the philosophy that all students should be prepared for postsecondary education upon graduation.

The school administration decided, for example, to offer no general math courses at Swansea High School, and Tech Prep students were strongly encouraged to take at least four math courses and three science courses by high school graduation. In addition, because the faculty and administrators agreed that competency in math does not begin at the secondary level, measures were taken to strengthen math in preceding grades. The district's long-term goal is to teach prealgebra to all seventh-grade students and algebra to all eighth-grade students.

These measures were not taken without extensive planning and some expectation for resistance. Teachers received extensive training and the opportunity for input at the annual Staff Development Conference sponsored by the Southern Regional Education Board staff. The movement toward interdisciplinary instruction and the teamwork between academic and vocational teachers strongly influenced the development of the curriculum.

After only two years of implementation, the high expectations for students in Lexington School District Four are paying off. The most recent dropout rate was only 1.03 percent, representing only six students. Test scores have improved, and the percentage of students transferring to a postsecondary institution has increased dramatically. The removal of the general track, with its inherently low expectations, has helped eliminate the sorting-machine nature of the traditional educational system. Lexington School District Four has one expectation for all students: every capable student is expected to acquire advanced skills in math, science, and communications. The combination of Tech Prep and college prep enables most students to accomplish this.

Issue #2: Developing a Smoothly Integrated Curriculum

In the past, college-prep programs at the secondary level have been designed to prepare students for academic achievement, while vocational programs have been geared more toward putting kids into jobs. (General-curriculum programs have not prepared secondary students for much of anything!)

The Tech Prep/Associate Degree curriculum, in contrast, is both academically and vocationally oriented. It prepares students to continue into postsecondary programs (especially into associate-degree programs), and it also provides them with sufficient job skills to perform well in the workforce. It offers a seamless, fully integrated course of study that smoothly combines academic and vocational content, using academics to build a foundation for vocational achievement and using vocational applications to reinforce academic concepts.

In designing and implementing such a curriculum, secondary schools have three major responsibilities:

1. to build (or rebuild) students' academic foundation,

2. to clearly identify and confirm students' future career paths and desired employment specializations,

3. to provide sufficient technical education/training to enable completers to enter the workforce after high school graduation or to move into the advanced academic and technical specialty courses without delays or course duplication.

In addition, some attention should ideally be given to the curriculum in the grades preceding the secondary school. Like Lexington School District Four, many schools systems that offer Tech Prep have benefited from introducing Tech Prep concepts into middle schools and even elementary schools. As early as kindergarten, for instance, students can benefit from contextually based instruction and integrated curriculum. And career counseling and exploration can begin much earlier than ninth grade. Some Tech Prep consortia place considerable emphasis on career counseling and exploration at the middle-school level; they find that this early career emphasis produces more motivated Tech Prep students.

The Pennsylvania College of Technology at Williamsport, Pennsylvania, in cooperation with high schools throughout the state and their business partners, has created a model for developing such an integrated Tech Prep curriculum. This model curriculum as illustrated in figure 1 emphasizes the importance

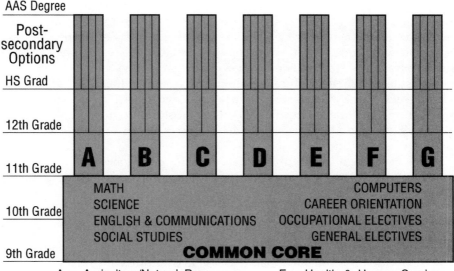

A = Agriculture/Natural Resources   E = Health & Human Services
B = Mechanical/Transportation   F = Construction & Design
C = Business & Computer Technologies   G = Communication Technologies
D = Engineering Technologies

Figure 1: Curriculum Structure Designed by Pennsylvania College of Technology

both of a solid academic foundation and of a career-cluster approach that allows students to progress from core subjects into broad career areas and finally to more focused career specialties. This concept of creating a foundation and building upon a foundation is the primary tool for creating flexibility and focus for Tech Prep students while they are still exploring and trying to decide where their interests and abilities lie.

In the ninth and tenth grades, all Tech Prep students take a common core curriculum consisting of applied math, science, and communications; social studies; computer literacy; and career orientation. Also possible are a few occupational and general electives. Beginning in the eleventh grade, students choose one of seven occupational clusters (agriculture/natural resources, mechanical/transportation, business and computer technologies, engineering technologies, health and human services, construction and design, and communication technologies). Some specialization may occur within a cluster in the twelfth grade, but the larger degree of specialization will occur in the postsecondary school, where advanced technical and academic courses are taken.

Issue #3: Determining Appropriate Outcomes

Redesigning the secondary curriculum to focus on a seamless transition from broad-based knowledge to specialized skills requires more than simply discussing course credits and requirements among secondary and post-secondary educators. In the past, high schools have easily slipped into an ivory-tower attitude about education—always gearing education require-ments toward the standards of higher education. Without arguing the age-old question of whether education should be a preparation for life or work, we can seek *both* by determining what skills and knowledge (outcomes or proficiencies) a student must be able to demonstrate in order to be a useful member of the workforce as well as an informed citizen and a well-rounded human being.

Some general outcomes, of course, will be common to all Tech Prep students. By the end of tenth grade, for instance, Tech Prep students should have:

- attained a high level of achievement in math, science, and communi-cations skills;

- decided or confirmed their decision to continue with Tech Prep; and

- selected an occupational/career cluster. (This selection will deter-mine the course of study for the eleventh and twelfth grades.)

By the end of twelfth grade, Tech Prep students should have:

- developed additional academic competencies;

- selected a specific career or technical specialty to pursue within their career cluster (At this point the students will have had some introductory technical courses and further counseling to help them in their decision.) ;

- attained clearly identified and recognized job-entry skills; and

- been accepted without deficiencies into the next phase of their education or training—either a postsecondary school, an apprenticeship program, or a job.

In addition to these general outcomes, however, each course of study will require a more specific set of competencies based on the particular needs of the business or industry that eventually will hire the Tech Prep graduate. Such competencies need to be determined through the input of industry and labor representatives.

In 1986, for example, Leander High School and Austin Community College identified and surveyed more than seventy businesses in the Austin, Texas, area for input before developing a sequence of competencies for an outcome-based curriculum in the instrumentation and control area of the engineering technology cluster. After considerable research into the employers' needs, a competency profile was developed that correlates job competencies and course content. This profile clearly identifies the specific outcomes expected of the instrumentation and control student at the end of both the secondary and postsecondary programs of study.

Later the high school also implemented a "career passport," a system in which Tech Prep students could keep a file of the competencies and demonstrated outcomes after they completed each year of their Tech Prep program. In addition to passing this record of competencies on to a postsecondary school, Tech Prep students can share their career passport with potential employers as proof of demonstrated abilities and accomplishments.

Issue #4: Connecting with Postsecondary Institutions

Creating a sequenced curriculum that opens doors for students rather than limiting them by tracking them or by failing to provide needed competencies is a vital concern for secondary institutions. Of equal importance, however, is keeping doors open for Tech Prep students *after* they leave the high school.

At present, the typical high school graduate in the general-education track does not immediately enter an associate-degree program. He or she is more likely to "go back to school" five to seven years later, when pressed by necessity to retrain or get a better job. But a secondary curriculum that provides a clear and open pathway to postsecondary education encourages students to go directly on to a community college and attain higher-level skills.

To provide this clear path from secondary to postsecondary education, the Tech Prep/Associate Degree curriculum must be sequenced in such a way that courses (and even more importantly, competencies) at the secondary school *articulate* or translate smoothly into a postsecondary program of study. Successfully completed courses taught at one institution must be recognized (and usually credited) by the other institution.

I have already discussed the concept of articulation earlier in this chapter and in chapter 5, but it might be helpful at this point to review the purposes of secondary/postsecondary articulation in a Tech Prep program. I found, in my view, one of the best definitions of articulation in 1978 from an unknown source:

> Articulation can be characterized as a process, an attitude, and a goal. As a process, it is the coordination of policies and practices among sectors of the education system to produce a smooth flow of students from one sector to another. As an attitude, it is exemplified by the willingness of educators in all sectors to work together to transcend the individual and institutional self-interest that impedes the maximum development of the student. As a goal, it is the creation of an educational system without artificial divisions, so that the whole educational period becomes one unbroken flow, which varies in speed for each individual, and which eliminates loss of credit, delays and unnecessary duplication of effort.[1]

Most early articulation agreements in vocational/technical programs made no attempt to achieve the kind of "unbroken flow" described in this definition. They were limited to equating content of technical courses offered in high school courses to similar courses offered by community or technical colleges in order to link the secondary and postsecondary curricula.

Tech Prep/Associate Degree programs, however, call for entirely new curricula that have been jointly designed by secondary faculty, postsecondary faculty, and employers. These programs reflect a clear plan for what a Tech Prep student should take in the secondary school and the logical continuation course sequence for postsecondary. This means, of course, that the postsecondary institution must accept (give credit for) the secondary classes—and be assured that the Tech Prep high school graduates are

---

1. After extensive research, the source for this definition remains unknown. If a source becomes available, we will indicate so in future publications.

adequately prepared for the advanced-skills program they should enter at a community college.

Such acceptance and assurance are by no means a foregone conclusion. In recent decades, postsecondary institutions and their faculty have become increasingly skeptical of assuming that a high school transcript represents any kind of significant accomplishment. In the academic areas, particularly, high schools have offered non-college-prep students weak alternative courses that present less content and require little in terms of student performance. The same has been true to a lesser degree for some technical courses.

For this reason—and others—articulation experiences have been more rewarding when secondary and postsecondary Tech Prep faculty have mutually agreed upon the *competencies* that a student must attain in the high school courses (rather than, for instance, the topics that must be covered). Such a practice is almost equivalent to having the two faculties jointly write—or approve—the final exams for the high school courses.

The Big Issue of University Acceptance

Another credit issue often raised between secondary and postsecondary schools relates to the ways that colleges credit high school applied-academics courses. Up until now, many community and technical colleges have been unwilling to give appropriate science and math credit to courses such as Principles of Technology and Applied Mathematics. Instead, they have given elective or vocational credit for these courses and then required the students to take the equivalent science and math courses at the community-college level. This results in a form of course redundancy that can be discouraging as well as expensive to students seeking to acquire advanced skills.

As we have seen, applied-academics courses differ from traditional courses in teaching method more than in content or achievement. Applied-academics courses stress the use of principles, laws, formulas, and rules in the real world as opposed to focusing on proofs of principles and laws, the deviation of formulas, and/or the evolution of rules. Nevertheless, studies show that students in applied courses achieve the same competencies as students enrolled in equivalent traditional courses. Community college administrators and faculty need to be persuaded of that fact so that students can be given appropriate credit for what they have achieved.

Incidentally, experience shows that who teaches the secondary course is an important factor in determining what kind of credit a postsecondary institution grants to an applied-academics course. Generally speaking, if an applied-science course is taught by a certified science teacher, it will more likely receive science credit than if it is taught by a vocational or industrial technology teacher.

Another important aspect of credit for applied-academics courses is their acceptance as meeting university entrance admissions requirements. Some

Tech Prep students who have taken applied courses have gained new confidence in themselves and new confidence in science and math and have therefore decided to pursue baccalaureate studies in science or engineering. To keep this option open, many schools and state education agencies have petitioned the universities to recognize the applied-science courses as meeting lab-science requirements for admission. Figure 2 shows a list of universities that recognize Principles of Technology as an acceptable lab science course.

By no means is the process of obtaining university recognition and acceptance for these courses a quick or easy task. In 1988, the North Shore School District and other secondary schools in Washington garnered the support of the Boeing Company (an active supporter of Tech Prep in the state) and the state superintendent's office and began a three-year journey to have Principles of Technology approved as an acceptable lab-science prerequisite at state universities. According to the rules of the Washington State Higher Education Coordinating Board, all six public four-year institutions had to unanimously accept the course before any of the institutions could recognize it. Despite resistance from one university in particular, the campaign for acceptance was ultimately successful, and three important components of the initiative paved the way for this success:

1. *The primary developer of the curriculum corresponded directly with the dean of the physics department at the resistant university to establish credibility of content.*

2. *The state launched an initiative for the Higher Education Coordinating Board to hear testimony from certified physics teachers who attested to the quality of the curriculum.*

3. *The Boeing Company provided strong and direct support throughout the process.*

Issue #5: Preparing Teachers for a New Role

Maintaining high expectations for high school students, integrating the content, focusing on outcomes, and smoothing the transition between secondary and postsecondary institutions are all important and necessary changes for the Tech Prep/Associate Degree curriculum. But curriculum changes are not enough to ensure effective education for high school students. When the classroom door closes, nothing new will take place without a teacher who is prepared and willing to teach new techniques and take on a new role.

ALABAMA
Alabama State University
Troy State University

COLORADO
Colorado State University

FLORIDA
Florida A&M University
Florida Atlantic University
Florida International University
Florida State University
University of Central Florida
University of Florida
University of North Florida
University of South Florida
University of West Florida

GEORGIA
University of Georgia

ILLINOIS
Illinois State University
Southern Illinois University

IOWA
Iowa State University

KANSAS
All four-year colleges and universities

MASSACHUSETTS
Massachusetts Institute of Technology
Northeastern University
Worcester PolyTech Institute

MINNESOTA
University of Minnesota

NEVADA
University of Nevada, Las Vegas
University of Nevada, Reno

NEW MEXICO
University of New Mexico

OREGON
Eastern Oregon State College
Oregon Health Sciences University
Oregon Institute of Technology
Oregon State University
Portland State University
Southern Oregon State College
University of Oregon
Western Oregon State College

TENNESSEE
East Tennessee State University
Memphis State University
Middle Tennessee State University
Tennessee State University
University of Tennessee at Chattanooga
University of Tennessee at Knoxville
University of Tennessee at Martin

TEXAS
Baylor University
Texas A&M University
Texas Tech University

VIRGINIA
Old Dominion University

WASHINGTON
Central Washington University
Eastern Washington University
Evergreen State College
University of Washington
Washington State University
Western Washington State University

**Figure 2. Universities that Recognize Principles of Technology
as an Acceptable Lab Science Course**

The Southern Regional Education Board in its most recent studies[2] has found that just handing teachers Tech Prep and applied-academics materials is not enough; they also need to be trained in contextual methods and given a chance to buy in to the entire process for change. Schools that have neglected this kind of teacher preparation have encountered powerful resistance to the Tech Prep initiative, plus failure on the part of the students and frustration on the part of the faculty.

Involving a selected number of teachers in designing the overall Tech Prep curriculum not only draws on their expertise in terms of content but also helps build teacher ownership in the program. And these teachers are often instrumental in influencing other teachers to give the new curriculum and methodology a chance.

One high school, for instance, began with a pilot program in applied academics. A few teachers were called upon to implement applied academics in only two classes. Soon those teachers were hooked on the concept; and their interest and excitement spread to other teachers within the high school and then to teachers at other high schools and in other school systems. By the end of the first year, most of the faculty in the district were ready to implement the applied-academics courses throughout the system.

Teachers who will be adopting applied academics or infusing contextual learning techniques should expect to spend anywhere from three days to two weeks in training sessions or workshops. Components of the training sessions should include:

- an overall understanding of contextual learning—the philosophies that undergird the methods;

- an overview of how the content has been reorganized to include applications and how applications reinforce the academic content; and

- an opportunity for individual teachers to modify the curriculum to meet state and local requirements and establish ownership of the program.

In 1991 the Goose Creek Consolidated Independent School District in Baytown, Texas, in partnership with Lee College and some of the largest petrochemical companies in the country, set out to completely reform their approach to curriculum and instruction in all grades from kindergarten to grade fourteen. Their goal has been to make all curriculum and instruction contextual within the next five to seven years. And they started their work

---

2. Gene Bottoms, Alice Presson, and Mary Johnson, *Making High Schools Work: Through Integration of Academic and Vocational Education* (Atlanta: Southern Regional Education Board, 1992), 191–92.

toward this goal by having a few teachers in the district begin using applied academics in the math, science, and language arts areas in one of the district's high schools. These teachers were trained to use the existing applied-academics curricula and then spent several weeks during the summer adapting the individual courses to fit state requirements for course credit and TAAS [3] requirements for standardized testing.

The teachers' excitement and success with this new approach to instruction spread so quickly that they were talking not only to other teachers within their school system, but also to many teachers and conferences across the state. The school system is now using its resources and approaches as a model in developing more applied resources in every discipline throughout the high school, middle school, community college, and even in the elementary schools. These educators, with strong support from the employers and the community, are breaking new ground in terms of curriculum development and educational transformation. They are actively committed to the philosophy that all students can learn if they are taught in appropriate ways and that they all should be exploring, experiencing, and preparing for a career throughout their education.

Issue #6: Requiring Students to Choose

Maintaining a curriculum and instructional delivery system that maintains student interest and adapts to student ability is critical to keeping students in school. Most high school dropouts are not leaving school because they cannot pass their courses; they are making a choice to abandon the educational system because they no longer believe it has a benefit in their lives. And they are making this choice at an early age; reports show that most students who drop out of school do so before the eleventh grade.

All students who enter high school are making choices (consciously or unconsciously) about their future. Some have chosen to work toward a university degree. Some have chosen to work after they graduate. But the majority (at least 50 percent) have unknowingly chosen a path to nowhere; they are choosing by *not* choosing. Drifting on the general track, they take the least rigorous courses available to obtain credit for high school graduation. Most of them are bored with school, and when they graduate they are prepared neither for further education nor for work at anything but no-skill or low-skill jobs.

Because all students are making choices anyway, it makes sense to help them make real choices that take them somewhere. Such choices are built in to the Tech Prep/Associate Degree curriculum. These are not choices that

---

3. TAAS, or Texas Assessment for Academic Skills, is a test required by the state for high school graduation.

limit opportunities, but educational and career choices that open doors. And they begin in the ninth grade, when students make the decision of whether or not to choose the Tech Prep curriculum.

In current practice, the nature of this choice varies from program to program. Many schools are now saying, "You must choose college (baccalaureate) prep or Tech Prep." Other school systems allow three choices: college prep, Tech Prep (leading to an associate degree or beyond) or "occupational prep" (leading to employment and sometimes apprenticeship immediately after high school).

Whatever the specific nature of the choice, it marks the beginning of a basic common core of course work that includes opportunities to explore careers through one-on-one counseling (involving the students and their parents), career-interest surveys, applied-academics courses, and perhaps contact with employers. Then, before entering the eleventh grade, Tech Prep students typically will make a further choice, selecting an occupational cluster such as health, engineering technology, or human services. After that decision, the career-awareness process continues through introductory technical courses, mentoring programs and worksite visits, and more counseling, all designed to help the student eventually choose a more specific career within the cluster.

None of these choices is irrevocable in a well-designed Tech Prep program. As we have seen, some students may change their minds and elect to move into a college (baccalaureate) prep plan. If the Tech Prep core courses in the ninth and tenth grades are appropriately designed, a shift into college prep should pose little problem for the student in terms of credits for high school graduation or college entrance.

The choices that students are asked to make in a school system that incorporates Tech Prep depend on how the schools within the Tech Prep consortium design their curriculum and establish their local goals. For instance, the Southern Maryland Education Consortium (SMEC) has three county school systems, each with a different set of choices for its students. All three school systems eliminated the general studies pathway and incorporated more rigorous academic courses into each career cluster area. However, each county school system established a slightly different set of choices for its students.

Charles County Public Schools, for instance, identifies a three-path system: Tech Prep, college prep, and occupational prep. Calvert County Public Schools, on the other hand, offers students the option of a traditional college-prep curriculum or one of two Tech Prep programs—either occupational or advanced program. St. Mary's County Public School System has opted for a single program with multiple pathways; ninth-grade students are asked to select a curriculum plan from four career clusters, one being a baccalaureate-prep program.

The Tech Prep initiative in Dothan, Alabama takes yet another approach to student choices. The program is based on the philosophy that education does not end with high school, that secondary education does not have a terminal goal, and that all students need to prepare for meaningful work, regardless of the path they take. All Dothan high school students therefore participate in a single program, called "Career Quest," which is structured on the Tech Prep model.

Each program of study is organized around a career cluster or strand designed to articulate with both the community/technical college and the four-year college programs. General vocational pathways have been eliminated; all studies lead to ongoing education and training and to usable job competencies.

Instead of deciding at the beginning of the program whether to attend a community college or university, students must select to pursue one of four career areas, industrial/engineering, health/human services, business information systems, and arts/humanities (often the college-prep, liberal-arts course of study). Many secondary schools that currently have a negative perception of vocational education have used this approach to meet the needs of their students and prepare them to work with emerging technology.

Issue #7: Anticipating Resistance

The high school components of Tech Prep discussed in this chapter are far-reaching and pervasive, requiring significant changes in technology, administration, curriculum, counseling, facilities, and policy. As I write, no Tech Prep consortium in the nation has completed all the required changes, but many are trying, and many have realized significant change in some areas. But this has not happened without resistance. Not everyone is convinced that Tech Prep belongs in our high schools, and establishing an effective secondary Tech Prep program must involve meeting resistance successfully.

Most of the resistance hinges on such issues as

- "turf"—Tech Prep is seen as a threat to jobs and authority,

- established practices—Tech Prep asks schools to adopt a different approach to teaching/learning, and

- false perceptions—Tech Prep is seen as just another fad, a way to "track" students or limit their options.

Faculty members, for example, may resist applied-academics courses because instituting these courses means making changes in both what is taught and how it is taught. Teachers may be skeptical about major departures from the way course content is presently organized; they may also feel they are being blamed for deficiencies in current programs or fear for their jobs if Tech Prep is adopted. But most teachers eventually prove willing to adopt new curricula if they truly improve student outcomes, and most are receptive to trying new materials and strategies if they are introduced to them by other teachers who have positive results.

Principals, counselors, and parents are the "gatekeepers" to student enrollment in Tech Prep. Their resistance is usually due to the perception that "this is just another alternative program" or the fear that Tech Prep may keep students from future options—particularly the opportunity to get a baccalaureate degree. These people are most likely to develop a positive attitude about Tech Prep and give the initiative their enthusiastic support and cooperation if they can be convinced that Tech Prep and applied academics really do open doors for students, giving them a reason for staying in school and a basis for achieving more in and out of school.

Superintendents, school boards, and other policymakers will at some point be asked to commit significant resources to pay for the laboratories, equipment, and teacher inservice required by Tech Prep initiatives. Federal grants are available for Tech Prep, but these funds are intended primarily to stimulate change and provide for planning/design and early implementation. Eventually, the price tag for ongoing Tech Prep programs will have to be borne by the school systems and included in the overall operating budget. Existing voc-ed budgets and corporate sponsorships likely will provide a portion of the funds needed. But a redistribution of existing resources may also be necessary, and this in turn may mean reducing the resources allocated for gifted/talented programs, special-education programs, or other initiatives. Such choices will be neither easy nor popular, but a strong case can be made for choosing a program that benefits the largest number of students.

Recognizing all these possible obstacles and dealing with them early are vital to making Tech Prep a success in secondary schools. And in one way or another, the strength for overcoming the barriers lies in a public-awareness campaign and broad-based support among all stakeholders in the community. In particular, the business community—the employers of future Tech Prep graduates—can play a crucial role in fostering acceptance by providing strong and useful support to the initiative. They—in addition to students—are the other big winners in this endeavor.

7

THE POST-SECONDARY

**Issues and
Answers for
Community
Colleges**

CHALLENGE

Look out community colleges! Change is coming in the form of a new student body. Your technical curriculum will never be the same—and that's good!

As I write in 1993, more than 650,000 students are enrolled in applied-academics courses taught at more than 23,000 high schools in all fifty states—and this number is growing by more than 75 percent each year. Upon high school graduation, at least half of these students will be showing up at the doors of technical and community colleges.

What will these students be like? They will be well prepared academically. They will know what kind of career they want to pursue. And they will expect the community college to anticipate their arrival with new courses and programs that will pique their interest, challenge their minds and skills, and deliver them—with an associate degree—to new job opportunities in a world-class workforce.

The next question becomes: Can the post-secondary institutions live up to those expectations?

More of these Tech Prep students will arrive at the community college immediately after high school graduation. This means that the average age of community college students could be much younger. It also implies that there should be a much larger percentage of full-time students, and more students will be taking the advanced courses and completing their associate degrees.

How can community and technical colleges prepare for Tech Prep students? What is the role of community and junior colleges in the Tech Prep/Associate Degree initiative? This chapter focuses on those questions as it describes eight issues involved with instituting and maintaining Tech Prep at the postsecondary level. Following a description of each issue, I provide an example to show how a Tech Prep consortium is addressing the issue.

Issue #1: Forging an Equal Partnership with Secondary Schools and Employers

Several years ago I invested in a real-estate development by becoming a member of a "limited partnership." Someone called a "general partner" had already put the plan together, found the real estate, and secured the loan. My job was easy; I just signed a few liability papers, cosigned the bank note, and sat back to reap the rewards of this deal that was just "too good to be true."

Within a few years, the bottom fell out of the real-estate market, and I quickly learned the real meaning of "too good to be true!" What I learned (and it was an expensive lesson) was that I had almost unlimited financial liabilities on this property but little or no control over how it was managed or what it produced.

Later, someone told me that my deal was not a true limited partnership. Nevertheless, I decided from that day forward that the only partnerships—of any kind—that I wanted were true partnerships in which the partners had equal commitment, equal voice (or control) and equal benefits or liabilities. With that kind of arrangement, if any one of the partners wins, all the partners win.

Unfortunately, many Tech Prep partnerships are also "limited partnerships." One partner puts the deal together and controls all the shots. The other partners just sign up for the liability. They don't call the shots or even participate in most decisions, and they don't see many of the benefits coming their way. Such a partnership tends to fall apart when problems arise and, usually nobody wins.

By virtue of being the senior institution in a Tech Prep/Associate Degree partnership and usually being the recipient of the grant funds, community colleges have the opportunity of being the lead partner and, if they so desire, can "call the shots." When this situation occurs—and it does occur all too often—the business partner becomes apathetic, the high school fails to attract the numbers or commitment from the Tech Prep students, and the community college feels no compulsion to make the curriculum and institutional changes that it needs to attract and keep students and transform them into tomorrow's workforce.

Strong, transforming Tech Prep initiatives happen when *all* the partners— high schools, community/technical colleges, and business/industry— operate as full partners. Such partnerships would mean that secondary schools, postsecondary institutions, and representatives of business and industry would work together (and with an equal voice) to

- develop the Tech Prep plan,

- design the curriculum,

- provide structures and support for Tech Prep program respectability and student recruitment and retention, and

- provide appropriate teaching and learning experiences to meet the expected outcomes for each course (providing the appropriate faculty, teaching materials, laboratories and equipment, work experiences, and student-support services).

In developing the curriculum, for example, employers would establish the program need and identify the skill standards for the Tech Prep jobs. Secondary and postsecondary educators then would work together to design the courses and sequences for the entire curriculum, setting up a smooth articulation between secondary and postsecondary phases. Finally, employers and educators would work together to ensure that the program meets both educational and workforce standards.

The Oakland County Tech Prep Consortium in Oakland County, Michigan, considers every partner in their consortium a key player on their planning and implementation teams. In fact, they purposely use the word team to illustrate the fact that all members are equal and necessary players. The various teams are developed on the basis of different Tech Prep components that need to be put in place, and each has established missions and objectives.

This strong emphasis on equal partnerships in Oakland County has yielded benefits ranging from new ideas for curriculum development to a new level of communication between secondary educators, postsecondary educators, and employers. Educators have developed a more global view of change by being pushed to consider the future results of improving the workforce and the effect on the community, the nation, and the world. And a "macro" view of planning has made faculty, administrators, and others aware of both the need for change and the potential for success.

Most of the educators and employers involved with the consortium claim that the newfound partnership is a beneficial and eye-opening experience. They are also taking full advantage of the potential for resource sharing among the partners. For example, community college faculty often teach workshops for high school teachers and also attend workshops offered by the secondary schools.

Even the Tech Prep director takes a partnership approach to her position, deliberately assuming a neutral view while facilitating and coordinating all facets of the consortium. Although her job has always been funded by the community college (not by grants), her office is housed at the Intermediate School District office (Oakland Schools). This arrangement helps give a sense of shared support and collaborative effort.

Issue #2: The Community's College's Place in the Middle of the Articulation

Although the standard Tech Prep articulation arrangement is a 4+2 plan (grades nine through twelve, plus two years in an associate-degree program), other combinations are possible as well. One possibility is a "4+2+2" articulation plan that would add on two years at a university culminating in a bachelor's degree. Chances are that only Tech Prep students would elect to follow this plan and complete a baccalaureate degree. But as long as the baccalaureate potential is available and a higher-level job is available commensurate with the additional education/training, keeping the 4+2+2 option open gives the program more potential and more respectability.

But maintaining a 4+2+2 articulation agreement brings a special set of challenges to community colleges, who find themselves "in the middle" of the articulation. They must recognize—and give credit for— appropriate secondary courses; they must also petition the four-year college or university to accept the community college's freshman/sophomore credits toward a baccalaureate degree. This may be a particularly sensitive issue for the community college's math and science faculty, who are aware of a tentative acceptance by their university colleagues and who are suspicious of being associated with any course that has the title *applied* in front. Nevertheless, several 4+2+2 Tech Prep models are emerging, and many others are in the exploration stages.

A carefully planned 4+2+2 articulation can yield tremendous benefits, providing students who never thought they could achieve higher education the opportunities and confidence to succeed. One highly effective example of such a program is run by the East San Gabriel Tech Prep Consortium in Los Angeles, California, a close partnership that includes a regional occupational center (secondary school) located in East San Gabriel Valley, the Los Angeles Trade Technical College, and California State University.

Students in East San Gabriel Valley are products of a typical low-income urban community with extremely high gang-related crime growing at the rate of approximately 74 percent each year. (This area was part of the area torn by riots in 1992.) More than 60 percent of these students come from single-parent families, and 80 percent are "latchkey kids." At the onset of the Tech Prep initiatives, the dropout rate was 54 percent, and most of the high school population had a grade point average of below 2.0.

Maribell was a typical student living in this community. At age fifteen, she was pregnant, felt unhappy with her life, and saw little hope for survival, much less a successful future. But Maribell's life began to turn around when a director of the regional occupational center talked with her about entering their Tech Prep fashion merchandising program.

When Maribell started the program she immediately became interested and involved in her courses. She also got a retail sales job through the program and soon became assistant manager of the store. She was so invested in the program that she missed only three days of school during the first year—to have her baby.

When she graduated, Maribell articulated her course work to Los Angeles Trade Technical School while continuing to work in retail. Now she has completed her associate's degree in fashion merchandising and plans to articulate into a bachelor's degree program at California State University, Los Angeles. Currently she is manager of a large retail store in Los Angeles and is happy with herself and her future.

Through the strong partnership of the three institutions and the dedicated efforts of the educators and employers involved in this Tech Prep initiative, many students in East San Gabriel Valley have been able to recognize their talents and interest in succeeding in an environment that offers little hope or opportunity. The curriculum in this program offers the applied-academics instruction, but the course structure has been adjusted to suit the needs of the region. The first priority of this consortium has been to get these students' immediate interest and involvement in a useful occupational program. When they pursue their studies to the technical college level, they are given the opportunity to build in more academic foundational courses for higher education.

These are students living in a very real and difficult world, and they need answers now. The three institutions involved in this articulated agreement recognize this need and are making a significant commitment to make sure that the students in this community can pursue higher education, get plugged into meaningful careers, and find a life worth living.

There have been many success stories like Maribell's as a result of the efforts of the East San Gabriel Valley Tech Prep initiative. With as many as three hundred Tech Prep students per class, the dropout rate has decreased to less than three percent. As many as 79 percent of the students who started the program have continued their studies like Maribell in a postsecondary institution, and more than 84 percent of the students are gaining employment while in the program or upon completion.

Issue #3: Reorganizing the Existing Curriculum

The postsecondary component of Tech Prep involves more than just admitting students from high school Tech Prep programs and giving them credit for applied-academics programs. It will usually be necessary, in order to serve students effectively, to replace the existing curriculum (or program) with a new Tech Prep curriculum. Tech Prep requires all participating schools—postsecondary as well as secondary—to find ways to reconstruct their curricula in order to build stronger foundations, increase competency levels, and provide opportunities for student choice.

There will be at least four reasons the existing curriculum will no longer be useful.

1. *It probably was designed to accommodate students with very poor academic foundations.* For several decades, postsecondary schools have been enrolling students with increasingly poorer math, science, and communications skills. This means that the college courses have had to be designed on the assumption that the student has little or no academic background. Many, therefore, are little more than skills training courses—inappropriate for the typical Tech Prep graduate.

2. *It is most likely out of date in terms of job competencies and employment needs.* A Tech Prep curriculum needs to provide knowledge/skills for future jobs in a new American workforce, not just reflect the current job market.

3. *It will likely contain academic courses that do not incorporate contextual learning methods.* (This is discussed under Issue #7.)

4. *It will probably not articulate smoothly with the core-skills, career-cluster approach adopted in the high schools.* As explained in chapter 5, this approach depends on first developing an overall Tech Prep curriculum, then deciding which parts of the curriculum need to be taught in secondary schools and which belong in postsecondary schools. (The high school portion of the Tech Prep curriculum will normally be derived from the common core while the community college segment will supply the specialty.)

Educators at Madison Area Technical College, in partnership with the public school system and several employers in Madison, Wisconsin, have been quite successful at reorganizing their curriculum to fit the Tech Prep approach; they call it the "Just in Time" approach. When the students complete their basic core curriculum and enter the curriculum common to their occupational cluster, they are considered to be in their second phase of "mapping" through the program (following the plan "mapped out" with their counselor, parents, and perhaps a teacher). From the students' point of view, they finish one phase "just in time" to enter the second phase—instead of killing time waiting to graduate.

The unique aspect of this curriculum is that it is built around competencies, not course sequence; that is, students finish the program when they can demonstrate a certain set of skills and knowledge, not when they have completed a certain sequence of courses. In addition, the competencies can be articulated from any high school to any community college within the state of Wisconsin. Local adaptations to the curriculum are usually made in the specialty areas, where employer demand may vary.

Issue #4: Providing Advanced Skills

With hundreds of new consortia forming across the country, Tech Prep practitioners are in a unique position to change education on many levels. Unfortunately, many of us are allowing one vital opportunity to pass us by. While significant changes are being made on the secondary level, the appropriate adjustment of postsecondary curriculum has faltered.

Tech Prep programs, in other words, are upgrading the skills of high school graduates but not the skills of those acquiring associate degrees. Skills are being enhanced at the high school level, and course repetition is being eliminated on the postsecondary level, but associate-degree requirements overall are not being changed. Community and technical colleges are not taking advantage of these students' stronger skills and of the instruction time made available by articulation with local high schools by offering technically advanced degree plans—or *advanced-skills* curricula.

The term *advanced skills* has sometimes been tossed around by educators, futurists, corporate specialists, economists, and sociologists with little regard for its real meaning or its implications for curriculum. So, what precisely does it mean in the context of a Tech Prep initiative? Simply put, an advanced-skills curriculum is one in which technical courses build upon the academic and technical content of prerequisite courses to enrich the degree program and provide the students with additional skills.

A well-constructed 2+2 (or 4+2) articulated program will eliminate redundant material (course work repeated at both secondary and post-secondary levels). The resulting savings in time can be used in one of two ways: the program may be either *time-shortened* or *skill-enhanced*. Time-shortened usually means that, under an articulation agreement, high school Tech Prep students may take equivalent postsecondary courses and, after graduation and entering a nearby postsecondary institution, receive credit for those courses, thereby completing an existing associate-degree program in less time. In time-shortened Tech Prep programs, requirements for the associate degree are essentially unchanged.

Describing a Tech Prep program as skill-enhanced, however, usually implies that the requirements for completing the associate degree have been raised. Students who receive postsecondary credit for their high school work would still go on to complete a full two-year postsecondary program, but this means they have more time to acquire additional competencies—or *advanced skills*. These can take any of several forms:

1. *Some advanced-skills programs provide more depth.* The most common interpretation of an advanced-skills curriculum is to describe it as providing more of the same, that is, a more thorough exposure to the field and more skills that build upon what has previously been learned. An example of including this form of advanced skills in a program for training telecommunications technicians would be the addition of courses in laser/fiber-optics communication links.

2. *Some advanced-skills programs provide more breadth,* such as cross-training. This form of advanced-skills program combines training in one specialization in high school with training for another at the postsecondary institution. (The student thus becomes competent in two different but related fields.) An alternative example could combine training in a particular specialty (such as construction) with training in business/management. It is likely that an apprenticeship program of some kind would be needed to provide construction experience and additional training.

3. *Some advanced-skills programs draw on the Tech Prep students' stronger academic background to teach more complex skills and knowledge.* In this approach, the learning of technical skills is enhanced by advanced courses that have a strong foundation in academic subjects such as math and science. Tech Prep students, with their background in applied academics, would have the background to benefit from such courses, while graduates of the traditional general track would likely be unable to handle the material.

An example from the electronics field will show the value of this third option and why it works only with a program like Tech Prep. Many secondary and postsecondary vocational-technical electronics programs currently being offered allow students to progress through several sequential electronics courses before they have completed algebra, trigonometry, and physics. The courses, therefore, must consist primarily of learning hand skills (such as soldering, wire wrapping, or calibrating equipment, memorizing certain facts about the way systems work, and learning certain trouble-shooting techniques) that are sure to become obsolete as the tools and technology advance. This type of beginning does not provide a foundation for learning advanced skills, nor does it provide the completer with the ability to learn, to solve problems, to create, or to innovate.

In Tech Prep, however, the use of applied-academics courses such as Principles of Technology provides the opportunity—by beginning in the ninth grade—to help the students build a solid math/science foundation while they are being introduced to technology. (This doesn't mean that hand skills and use of lab equipment should not be taught; it just means that teaching these skills should be complimentary to teaching the academic foundation.) The postsecondary schools can then continue to strengthen this foundation by introducing new analytically based and scientifically based electronics courses.[1]

It is a natural progression of supply and demand to move toward advanced skills in a Tech Prep curriculum. The better-prepared, more flexible students as a result of Tech Prep on the secondary level automatically demand that postsecondary schools upgrade their instructional offerings, and so do employers for graduates with more advanced skills. It is up to postsecondary schools to respond with the kind of high-quality, high-skills instruction that the changing workforce demands.

One of the Tech Prep consortia catching that vision is the Partnership for Academic and Career Education (PACE) a three-county Tech Prep initiative in South Carolina. For years, PACE has offered an advanced-placement program whereby high school seniors who have demonstrated certain competencies are allowed to earn Tri-County Technical College credit based on their demonstrated technical and academic competencies. Prior to the 1990–91 academic year, however, postsecondary curriculum development in the PACE program was limited to reviewing entry-level skills and smoothing the transition from the secondary to the postsecondary level of education through the articulation process. In the fall of 1990, however, the college faculty and the PACE staff moved toward an advanced-skills model by developing "advanced-technology certificates" to enable Tech Prep students to graduate with two postsecondary credentials in the time normally required to finish an associate degree.

The PACE curriculum and program implementation have been recognized by organizations such as the American Association of Community Colleges and the United States Department of Education as one of the best Tech Prep models in the country. It is certainly proving popular with its own students.

1. A Tech Prep program with this type of advanced-skills curriculum addresses many of the issues described in the report prepared by the Secretary's Commission on Achieving Necessary Skills (SCANS), *What Work Requires of Schools* (Washington, DC: Government Printing Office, 1992) and Commission on the Skills of the American Workforce, *America's Choice: High Skills or Low Wages* (Rochester, NY: National Center on Education and the Economy, 1990).

During the 1992–93 school year, 4,254 students—a third of the total students enrolled in grades nine through twelve—were enrolled in Tech Prep programs in the PACE consortium's sixteen high schools/career centers. And postsecondary enrollment in Tech Prep continues to grow each year as the students graduate from the secondary half of the program and continue their education at Tri-County Technical College.

Issue #5: Bridging the Gap for Adult Students Without Tech Prep

If the competencies of today's Tech Prep high school graduates and the needs of today's employers call for an advanced-skills curriculum, why aren't more postsecondary institutions changing their curricula to offer such a plan? The simple answer lies in numbers. Tech Prep graduates, while growing rapidly in number, still make up a relatively small percentage of the postsecondary student population.

At present, the average student entering a community- or technical-college system is twenty-eight years old and has not had the benefit of Tech Prep in high school. This means the colleges have had to focus up to a third of the curriculum on providing academics and basic technology for these students. Postsecondary institutions at this point are reluctant to upgrade their programs until a sufficient demand is placed upon them by increased numbers of qualified students.

For the next five years, less than one third of the postsecondary enrollment will consist of students who have completed the high school portion of Tech Prep. And until secondary Tech Prep programs are more fully implemented, most incoming postsecondary students will not be qualified for advanced-technology courses—and colleges will not be motivated to offer advanced-skills programs.

What is needed to get around this waiting game is a transitional level of course work at the postsecondary level. Advanced skills could be taught at all community and technical colleges if a "bridge" program were put in place to bring non-Tech-Prep graduates up to speed in the same basic technology and academics the Tech Prep graduates have been taught in high school. Meanwhile, high school Tech Prep graduates would be able to bypass the bridge program and proceed directly into an advanced math/science and core technical skills program. These students would thus be able to complete a new level for advanced skills or cross-training within the traditional two-year time frame.

A Tech Prep bridge program for a technical field should contain the essential content of applied-academics courses such as Principles of Technology, Applied Mathematics, Applied Communication, and in some fields Applied Biology/Chemistry. It would also contain more work-related courses such as Use of Personal Computers and Quality Control Concepts/Practices.

Transformations (Tech Prep for Adults) is a bridge program designed by CORD to support a Tech Prep/Associate Degree plan. It consists of two quarters or one semester of college work containing the essential elements of a high school Tech Prep program, and it features almost six hundred contact hours of rigorous training in applied academics and basic technology.

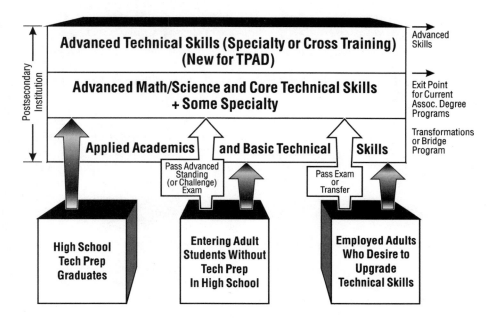

Figure 1. How Does a "Bridge Program" Fit Into a Tech Prep Curriculum?

A Tech Prep bridge program such as Transformations can be adapted in various ways to fit the specific needs of students and colleges. For instance, offering advanced-standing exams instead of automatically requiring "bridge" course work would allow more advanced students (perhaps those who have baccalaureate degrees but are returning to school to learn a technical specialty) to avoid repeating course work that was familiar to them. The choice of entering the Tech Prep bridge program for one semester or passing the advanced-standing exam leading directly into advanced math/science course work would meet the needs of a wide variety of individual experience and skills levels.

Even if Tech Prep students are not yet the majority in our community and technical colleges, it is time for these institutions to respond to their needs and to the needs of the marketplace. Advanced skills are the answer, and a Tech Prep bridge program provides the means. Through it the community/technical-college system can continue to serve all sectors of the entering population while carrying out the mission of Tech Prep—preparing the much-needed technically advanced workforce for our country and our future.

At this point, several bridge programs have begun to emerge across the country in conjunction with the Tech Prep initiative, and these programs are enjoying significant success. Texas State Technical College (TSTC) in Waco, Texas, began its bridge program to retrain displaced adult workers so they could reenter the workforce, and they soon discovered that the bridge program produced a solid educational foundation on which these adult learners could build a technical specialty. (It has been used successfully with high school graduates as well.)[2]

The teaching methodology provides both a major benefit of this program and a primary reason for its success. Students are in class from eight in the morning until five in the evening, five days a week for twelve weeks (this is to meet the quarter system). This concentrated method of delivery tends to restructure the students' learning habits. Peer support is encouraged, and students team up and approach problems as a group. In addition, accessible (open) labs and contextual teaching methods have helped the students achieve the stated outcomes. TSTC has benefited from this program because the instructors in the institution's forty-five different program areas receive better, more-prepared students.

In Hamilton, Alabama, the Northwest Community College has used a similar approach both for adults and for recent high school graduates who did not have the opportunity to enroll in Tech Prep. Jump Start is a program designed to bridge the gap between existing high school content and basic technology required for success in a technical field. It consists of two quarters of college work in which the students study Principles of Technology and Applied Mathematics as well as Engineering Graphics, Computer Usage, and Fundamentals of Electricity and Electronics. In addition to these core courses, Jump Start includes a class called World of Work, which focuses on the job market.

Issue #6: A Competency-Based Curriculum That Looks Forward

As we have seen, Tech Prep/Associate Degree is a competency-based curriculum aimed at producing graduates who have the skills employers need. But in determining what these skills are, it's important to think toward the future, not simply duplicate the skills and characteristics of the current

---

2. For further information on this program, see Steve Malbrough, "A Technology Boot Camp in Texas" in Dan Hull and Dale Parnell, *Tech Prep/Associate Degree: A Win/Win Experience* (Waco, TX: Center for Occupational Research and Development, 1991), 221–29.

workforce. Tech Prep curricula, especially at the postsecondary level, need to provide skills for the workforce in the last half of this decade and beyond. After all, since the very nature of the Tech Prep curriculum (it takes six years!) indicates that it will be a while before Tech Prep workers permeate the workforce, curriculum designs need to project at least that far forward.

In light of this need for forward-looking competencies, there should be a concern that typical methodologies for designing competency-based curricula (such as examining today's jobs and talking to first-level supervisors) tend to replicate what currently exists. Employers tell us that they want something new and better. To ensure this, new advanced-skills curricula should be designed by making use of industry's managers who have sufficient vision to project their needs four to six years in advance.

Even without these strategies, it's not hard to predict that, in the future, most jobs that offer growth, challenge and earning potential require a working knowledge of mathematical and technical principles and adequate communications skills. By building the foundation on these skills early in high school and by using this foundation in subsequent course work, it is possible to ensure a wide choice of job capabilities for all future workers. Coupled with forward-looking occupationally specific competencies, this foundational approach can provide the greatest educational value to the largest number of students.

Issue #7: Bringing Contextual and Applied Learning into the Postsecondary Schools

Hands-on learning has been the mainstay of vocational and technical education for more than four decades. "Learning by doing" has proven to be an effective technique for skills training, job training, creating interest in school, showing relevance of educational training to problems in the real world, and developing confidence through developing manual dexterity. But until the mid 1980s, hands-on learning was primarily reserved for alternative education in which "ungifted" students were thought to have no potential for head skills.

As we have seen, this notion has been soundly discredited in recent years. Cognitive science indicates that humans have multiple forms of intelligence and multiple learning styles, and contextual learning methods can be far more effective in teaching the majority of learners than the abstract methods traditionally employed in postsecondary institutions.

Despite the success of curricula based on contextual approaches, however, many teachers remain resistant to trying such an approach—and getting faculty to change the ways they teach is much more of a challenge at the community college than it is at the high school. There are at least three reasons for this resistance:

1. Postsecondary faculty are much more independent and usually function with far less supervision. (It's harder to *make* them teach in a certain way.)

2. Relatively few examples of postsecondary curriculum materials support contextual or applied learning. (I will mention a few at the end of this section.)

3. The driving force for most academic faculty at community colleges is student preparation—and course credit—for the upper division programs at universities, where almost all subjects are keyed to abstract learning.

Despite these reasons for resistance, it's time for contextual learning to take its rightful place in postsecondary classrooms. By 1995, more than five hundred thousand high school Tech Prep students will be graduating and over half of them will be arriving at community colleges. These students will be mostly contextual learners, and they will have completed the secondary portion of their Tech Prep curriculum in part because they found the courses interesting, meaningful, and achievable. Other students, non-Tech-Prep graduates, will stand a far better chance of succeeding in their studies if they are taught by contextual methods.

What is the best strategy for overcoming resistance to contextual teaching and meeting the needs of these incoming students?

1. Faculty must be convinced that contextual learning strategies are effective and can be implemented. This can best be done by giving the teachers themselves an opportunity to learn contextually and perhaps giving them a few examples (an exercise, lab, or scenario) that they can use in their classes.

2. Existing academic courses should be modified to incorporate contextual content and teaching strategies. Completely new courses and course materials will be very difficult to develop within the needed time frame. Furthermore, new curricula are not likely to be adopted easily, and four-year colleges and universities may be reluctant to accept credits from community colleges for new, nontraditional courses.

3. Faculty must be empowered to make the contextual changes in their courses—through workshops, release time for development, and networks for exchanging useful innovations.

In their efforts to encourage more contextual instruction at the postsecondary level, the Community College of Rhode Island is currently working with the university schools of education and the higher education board to include contextual teaching strategies into teacher education programs. In addition, this college is already placing an emphasis on selecting teachers who have a knowledge of and practice these types of techniques.

Contextual/Applied Learning Curricula for Postsecondary Schools

As I have mentioned, relatively few postsecondary curricula have been developed or designed using contextual/applied learning strategies. I am aware, however, of at least three courses that are currently in use and enjoying significant success:

Unified Technical Concepts and Physics for Technicians: A Systems Approach

These two postsecondary physics courses are an appropriate next step for students who have taken Principles of Technology. Like their secondary counterpart, these courses feature labs and hands-on discovery and focus more on principles and application than on derivations and proofs. They also attempt to make connections for the student between the basic quantities of physics in the various energy systems—mechanical, fluid, electromagnetic, and thermal—and to show how they apply to the maintenance, modification, and repair of complex technical systems. As appropriate for a postsecondary course, however, they require higher-level math skills.

Unified Technical Concepts has been used in postsecondary technical training programs since 1978 and has been well received. (In fact, this course provided the framework for the development of Principles of Technology and for Physics for Technicians: A Systems Approach.) One of the chief strengths of this course is emphasis on laboratory experience. The application modules provide a hands-on learning experience that is more useful to the technician than the "blackboard approach" used in most traditional physics courses.

Physics for Technicians, developed in response to requests from teachers who had been using Unified Technical Concepts, retains the basic format and philosophy of the first course (including the laboratory emphasis) but features an upgraded content. It is designed to take advantage of the better preparedness of students entering postsecondary schools from Tech Prep programs and is therefore an ideal course for students who have completed Principles of Technology. Physics for Technicians upgrades the math content to a precalculus level; adds more equations and more derivations; includes study of magnetism, optics, and lasers; and increases the number of exercises for students.

Secondary/Postsecondary Articulation of Mathematics at Mt. Hood Community College

In 1991, Mt. Hood Community College in Gresham, Oregon set out to design a single track of mathematics courses for students enrolling in entry-level mathematics at the college level and high school level. The curriculum is designed into four levels of mathematics but the students work through the levels at their own pace. This vertical integration of technical mathematics and college-prep mathematics has made it possible for Tech Prep and baccalaureate-prep students to experience the applied/contextual learning techniques at the secondary level, and the Tech Prep high school graduates continue this learning at the postsecondary level when entering Mt. Hood Community College. Those non-Tech Prep graduates who enter the community college can also enter one of the four levels of the mathematics so that they do not lose any foundational concepts. The faculty at the community college and high schools felt that all students should experience the same prerequisite mathematics.

Pamela Matthews, the Associate Dean of Mathematics and primary designer of this curriculum, has worked hard to practice the philosophy that mathematics can be meaningful to students if it is taught in a contextual or interactive manner. She and other members of the college have made significant strides towards changing the teaching methods at the college and remain consistent with the mission and standards of the National Council of Teachers of Mathematics.

Postsecondary Articulation of Applied-Academics Curricula in Seattle

South Seattle Community College has been working with the Seattle Public Schools and the Boeing Company for more than two years to design completely articulated secondary/postsecondary curricula in technical fields such as electronics. These curricula begin in high school with the applied-academics courses described in chapter 4, including Applied Mathematics, Principles of Technology, Applied Communication, Applied Biology/Chemistry, and Applied Humanities. And the community college is attempting to use or create higher-level applied-academics courses that build on the competencies developed in these high school courses. For instance, they are teaching Physics for Technicians as a postsecondary articulated advancement to Principles of Technology. They are also working to create technical communications courses to articulate with the Applied Communication high school course and higher-level math courses to build on Applied Mathematics. The Applied Humanities courses are being taught at both the secondary and postsecondary levels.

Similar efforts are underway to develop a seamless (secondary/postsecondary) articulation for the technical courses by building the high school courses on the scientific foundation provided by Principles of Technology and designing advanced-skills courses at the community college that build on the introductory courses in high school.

This highly ambitious effort toward complete vertical and horizontal articulation in a Tech Prep curriculum is still in its early stages, and many issues remain to be resolved. But through the vision and persistence of leaders like Dr. Gerald Butts, Vocational Director of Seattle Public Schools, and Dr. Jerry Reel, Dean of Technology at South Seattle Community College, the program is evolving in a most impressive manner. The Boeing Company, which has provided significant financial and technical support for this development, has extended its efforts to providing summer internships for faculty and apprenticeship experiences for students. This aspect of the program will be described further in the next chapter.

Issue #8: Increasing Postsecondary Commitment to Tech Prep

More than half of the Tech Prep high school completers are expected to continue as full-time students in community colleges. The question is whether the community colleges are prepared to offer these students meaningful, challenging programs that are logical extensions of their high school experience.

Unfortunately, according to my observation, this is not the case with most community colleges at the present time. In fact, as far as I can tell, most community colleges do not appear to be affected much by Tech Prep. They seem much more concerned with articulating existing students and programs into the universities than they are with creating new opportunities and pathways for high school students entering and graduating from associate-degree programs.

Despite evidence that a closer linkage with high school curricula will create stronger course offerings at the community college level, many community college educators seem stuck in the notion that the tie with high schools will water down curriculum and create less credibility (or "creditability") with higher education. Tech Prep is seen by most community college educators as falling in the "voc-ed side of the house," and this perception causes some academic faculty to hesitate about participating in Tech-Prep-style articulation and applied teaching methods.

In recent years, an increasing number of community college presidents have proved willing to represent their institutions as strong, visible advocates of Tech Prep/Associate Degree. They have encouraged their faculty to welcome this initiative as an opportunity, not an imposition. Their efforts are paying off in terms of strong, productive programs.

Unfortunately, these forward-looking postsecondary educators are still in the minority. As I write, relatively few community colleges have changed their curricula in response to Tech Prep. (The program at South Seattle Community College, described in the previous section, is a wonderful exception.) Course-by-course "articulation," whereby students in eleventh and twelfth grades take courses for which they will receive postsecondary credits, remains the only involvement many community colleges offer with the high schools. And this must change for Tech Prep to fulfill its potential as a true educational reform.

Granting credit through articulation is neither the strength nor the potential of Tech Prep. Getting students through school as quickly as possible is not the point; neither is getting all community college students into the university. A more appropriate objective for the majority of students is to provide them with a smooth, seamless and logical transition from high school to community college and beyond—and an opportunity to acquire the advanced skills they need to excel in tomorrow's workplace.

To achieve the benefits of Tech Prep, community colleges will need to commit to the following:

- significant curriculum reform, changing from low-level, time-short-ened, articulated programs, to a full two-year, advanced-skills Tech Prep curriculum;

- strong, equal partnerships with high schools and businesses (future employers);

- strong, equal partnerships between academic and technical faculty;

- significant outreach to high schools and career-guidance support; and

- partnerships with four-year institutions to provide Tech Prep/Associate Degree completers an opportunity to articulate into baccalaureate programs.

The results of such a commitment will be many. Community and technical colleges will find themselves with larger enrollments. (This may bring problems in the short term but should prove beneficial over the long haul.) They will attract better-prepared students with stronger academic competencies and a clearer vision of what they want—and more of these are likely to be full-time students who go on to complete their degrees.

Colleges that commit to Tech Prep will enjoy excellent opportunities for improving public relations and establishing long-term relationships with high schools, businesses, and the community; they will also be enabled to upgrade their curricula and teach more advanced skills. Most important, colleges have a chance to play a vital role in an initiative that, for many Americans, is the key to opening minds and opening doors into the future. If community colleges don't change it is likely that they will not be seen by some as the deliverers of the advanced-skills phase of Tech Prep.

The federal Carl Perkins Tech Prep legislation provides an alternative for high school completers to articulate into an apprenticeship program instead of continuing their studies at a community college. Some would argue that this is a more realistic route because community colleges are not creating the new, advanced-skills curriculum that Tech Prep students need.

I disagree with this "either-or" (re-enroll or apprenticeship) line of thinking, partly because I believe that more community colleges will improve or upgrade their curricula when they are receiving more Tech Prep students and partly because "lighthouse examples" like South Seattle Community College are already paving the way for the new community college role in Tech Prep.

The best of all scenarios, in my opinion, is a combined postsecondary/employer program in which community colleges and businesses work together to provide a coordinated, complementary mix of school-based learning and worksite learning. This may be the ultimate form of integration—*the school-work integration model.* In the next chapter, I discuss in more depth the employers' role in such a model.

8.

A NEW BUSINESS

The School-Work Integration Model

EDUCATION PARTNERSHIP

Three elements, taken together, distinguish Tech Prep/Associate Degree from other education initiatives and training programs:

- Tech Prep is based in the belief that *all* its students need a solid academic foundation—and can learn higher-level academic material if it is taught the right way.

- Tech Prep promotes a seamless linkage between secondary and post-secondary education.

- Tech Prep clearly aims at preparing students for employment in a chosen field.

This third element, employment preparation, takes on entirely new implications in light of recently evolving national goals and the need for a newly structured and differently prepared workforce. To remain competitive in a world market (and to keep jobs in the United States), American employers need more than compliant assemblers, clerks, and craftspersons. They need creative, problem-solving, flexible workers who know the foundations, tools, skills, and techniques of the new jobs. Ideally, they need people who already have work experience in their chosen fields.

It is doubtful that the existing educational institutions in the United States have the entire capacity and possess sufficient know-how to prepare this new workforce. Our present system, as we have seen, has been primarily geared to either funneling students toward universities; giving them specific, inflexible job skills; or providing them with a watered-down, "general" education that prepares them for neither work nor future education.

Neither can we reasonably expect (as some pundits have recommended) to simply borrow another country's education and training system and put it in place in our own culture. An examination of European partnerships between education, employer, and labor organizations, for instance, reveals at least the capacity for delivering the appropriate education and training (if the content and curriculum were properly designed), and these groups have some history of working together. However, the educational environment, business culture, and governmental leadership in the European community are so different from the United States that our attempts to recreate similar educational partnerships likely would meet with very limited success.

What we need is to create our own, hybrid partnership between educators, employers, and labor to share responsibilities for building a world-class workforce. And Tech Prep/Associate Degree provides an ideal place to begin in forging such a partnership.

What Is the Employer's Role?

Our nation's history of employer involvement in career-oriented educational programs has at best been spotty, sporadic, and minimally effective. Most vocational and technical education programs at secondary and postsecondary levels have involved some sort of advisory committee that provided input about what should be taught and that tacitly approved the curriculum. But in many instances these advisory committees have consisted primarily of retired workers, adjunct professors, government representatives, and job incumbents—not nearly enough future employers. And their responsibilities have often been limited to concurring on a curriculum that *educators have already created*, volunteering to speak to students about their work, and donating worn-out or obsolete equipment.

Employers are at least partly to blame for this problem of minimal employer involvement because of their lack of assertiveness and, in some cases, their unwillingness to commit time and resources to participate fully. Even though they often complain about educators' lack of responsiveness to their needs, employers rarely are motivated to give much more than occasional advice. They seem to feel that the education/training of their workers will somehow just happen, and they do not place a sufficiently high priority on this effort to justify expending much time beyond annual or semiannual advisory-committee meetings. The dominant attitude is, "After all, we Americans pay taxes so that other people are paid to worry about public education for us."

But some employers today are realizing that the education picture hasn't improved in recent years and that just complaining about it and paying taxes will not be enough to establish a stronger workforce. They are also realizing that if they do not put the time and money into pre-employment education and training efforts such as Tech Prep, they will be forced to continue investing heavily in employer-sponsored educational remediation and second-chance training programs for their employees. Because of these realizations, they are opening their minds to the possibilities of Tech Prep and opening their doors to the delivery of the training aspects of the curriculum.

So what is to be the employer's new role in Tech Prep/Associate Degree programs? There is no single, simple answer to this question; it depends on the employer's size, health, mission, and needs and the educational institution's structure, field of specialization, and level of student achievement. The particular support or input that one employer might contribute to a Tech Prep program will also depend on the interest and commitment of the individual who represents the organization or creates the initiative. But the overall role of the employer in a Tech Prep partnership should include some voice, responsibility, authority, or directed activity in the following:

- content (identifying what material the Tech Prep curriculum/courses should cover),

- needs/outcomes (establishing the skills and knowledge Tech Prep graduates should possess at various stages of completion),

- form of employer support (identifying ways in which employers can assist with the Tech Prep curriculum and be responsible for how it is delivered), and

- review and assessment (evaluating student outcomes and program quality and determining whether the program is effectively addressing the needs of all concerned).

More specifically, the employer's role in Tech Prep should address at least eight issues, which we will explore in this chapter. Note, however, that this is not a complete list of the activities that include some kind of employer involvement. Nor does it fully explain the depth of involvement or the amount of say that employers should have in educational decisions. While employers need to have input in Tech Prep curriculum, they should not necessarily have the last word on how it is designed and taught.

Issue #1: Establishing a Policy Demand on the System

Tech Prep is not the only reform available in the educational marketplace. Every year, many worthwhile (or not so worthwhile) initiatives are proposed. And not everyone in the educational community is convinced that

Tech Prep is the way to go. Some people may view it as just another fad . . . or as a new, glitzy name for an old idea such as tracking or vocational education. As a result of such competition and misconceptions, long-term interest in and continued funding for Tech Prep may be hard to come by.

The inducement for the educational community to explore new programs or initiatives such as Tech Prep is typically a response to receiving support and/or funding from various education agencies. Appropriately, grants stemming from federal legislation and some state appropriations are available to be used for Tech Prep programs. However, such funding is usually intended as "seed money" for planning, design, and initial implementation. Long-term support for continuation and growth of a Tech Prep program will need to come from local institutional budgets; that is, the school systems and colleges will need to foot the bill.

Because school districts and community colleges are usually faced with tight operating budgets, securing funding for new initiatives will usually mean reducing the amounts of existing budget items or eliminating other programs altogether. Setting a higher priority on Tech Prep and its benefit to middle-quartile students—which may mean setting a lower priority on others—is a significant policy decision for administrators and governing boards of educational institutions. Such policy changes are unlikely to be enacted without some sort of external demand. And thus far the most effective "demanders" of Tech Prep are economic development organizations and the business community—the future employers of Tech Prep students.

The Cypress-Fairbanks Independent School District, located near Houston, Texas, has found its partnership with the Cypress-Fairbanks Chamber of Commerce of immense value in maintaining its Tech Prep initiatives. The initial Tech Prep planning carried out by the schools' administrators and the chamber's education committee resulted in several positive initiatives for Tech Prep. Then, when the school board set out to find a new superintendent, the chamber stepped in with some suggestions. In a presentation to the school board, highly respected members of the community and representatives of the chamber of commerce publicly asked the school board to consider a superintendent who had a knowledge of, interest in, and commitment to the Tech Prep philosophy. As a result, the superintendent hired continues to provide support and commitment to Tech Prep.

However, the chamber's involvement and work with the school system did not stop there. Les Robertson, Director of Human Resource Development for Cooper Industries, the largest employer in Houston, and other members of the chamber education committee set aside time to meet with the school personnel to discuss outcomes, curricula, and the kinds of standards needed for students to become a vital and contributing factor in the local workforce. Today, the

Cypress-Fairbanks Chamber of Commerce and the Cypress-Fairbanks Independent School District are still a strong and thriving partnership not only in Tech Prep, but also in many other initiatives.

Issue #2: Establishing the Need for a New Workforce

Most of the vocational and technical educational programs delivered by high schools and community colleges were developed several decades ago and have changed only slowly and slightly as added faculty, new equipment, and changing enrollments have dictated modifications. In most communities, the basic thrust of these existing programs remains unchanged; they are designed to accept students with poor academic achievement and their curriculum content slants toward providing skills training in narrow specialties.

Most Tech Prep consortia begin by attempting to modify these traditional vocational-technical programs. Courses are articulated from secondary to postsecondary levels and applied-academics courses are added, but the content and level of the technical courses do not typically reflect the advanced level of the students in their knowledge of math, science, and basic technical principles. As earlier chapters have already made clear, such modified programs will not be sufficient to provide the kind of employees that employers need to stay competitive. And employers, working with community and school leadership can be instrumental in getting this message across. They can do this by clearly identifying their workforce needs and showing why new, advanced-skills Tech Prep/Associate Degree curricula must be designed and implemented to prepare employees for the workforce.

Clark M. Greene, Manager of Training at Georgetown Steel Corporation, expresses his concerns and hopes on how Tech Prep can address the needs of the workforce in his letter to the National Tech Prep Network (shown on the following page).

Issues #3: Establishing Respectability and Recruiting New Students

In many communities Tech Prep suffers from a "perception liability," which in plain terms means that some people think it is a second-rate program aimed at second-rate students. This attitude stems from two common misconceptions:

- the mistaken idea that because Tech Prep is directed primarily at the non-baccalaureate-bound, it therefore expects less from its students, and

- the false assumption that applied-academics courses are watered-down and less-than-credible versions of "real" academic subjects.

GEORGETOWN STEEL CORPORATION

P.O. Box 619
Georgetown, S.C. 29442
803/546-2525 Telex 805053

February 14, 1993

To Members of the National Tech Prep Network:

I first became involved in Horry/Georgetown Tech Prep in May of 1992, but in actuality I have been involved with the technical education field for many years. Through my background in industry, both as an hourly employee and manager, as well as my education at the college/technical college level, I have had the opportunity to see Tech Prep from more than a one-sided view.

If Tech Prep is to prosper, we (business, industry, schools, and students) need to reap the benefits equally. We want people prepared, equipped to work, and ready to learn—*continually*. While these relationships [between educators and employers] are yet in the beginning stages, we are making progress as "partners." We must understand what this alliance represents.

I think that business/industry has the distinctive role of being both a supplier and a customer of the school systems. We will be the end users of this change and as such must make sure our needs are known. Our needs expand and change constantly, and if we do not maintain adequate communication to relay that information we will be the loser. Business and industry received their "wake-up call" during the 1980s; it's time that the education system recognized their segment of responsibility [for providing a world-class workforce]. We can be a valuable resource to our schools and long ago should have made ourselves more accessible to the people that equip the employees of the future.

Shame on you, educators, for not knocking on our door—and shame on us for not knocking on yours. It's time to put our differences aside and move forward in this exciting new initiative. I believe that we have an obligation to our communities in assisting this system to better respond to our ever-changing needs.

Sincerely,

Clark M. Greene
Manager of Training

As we have seen, neither of these ideas is true. However, misperceptions can be powerful shapers of attitude and response. The idea that Tech Prep is a second-rate program could severely limit its attractiveness and recruitment potential to middle-quartile students. Yet such mistaken ideas about Tech Prep can be (and in many instances have been) dismissed by strong, visible, and vocal support of Tech Prep from the employers.

Employer support of Tech Prep can take many forms. Through editorials, pamphlets, public-service speeches, talks at PTA meetings, and radio/television news spots, potential employers can speak in favor of Tech Prep and thus give the program a powerful boost. They can state that they will hire and are hiring Tech Prep graduates. When practical, they can even announce the jobs and compensation ranges that are available to Tech Prep/Associate Degree graduates and explain the career ladder these graduates can expect to climb.

Doug James, the Superintendent of Schools in Richmond County, North Carolina, attributes much of the student motivation and interest in the Richmond County Tech Prep initiative to the vocal support of businesses and industry in the area. When the Tech Prep initiative was first being marketed in the area, for example, employer representatives conducted large and small group meetings with students to impress on them the benefits and importance of Tech Prep/Associate Degree. Breakfast meetings were also held to update business and industrial executives on the progress of the Tech Prep program and to provide marketing materials for them to distribute to their employees (parents of potential Tech Prep students).

Employer support for the Richmond County initiative took many different forms and came from many different directions. The Greater Richmond County Chamber of Commerce endorsed Tech Prep and included the program in promotional material. A local foundation offered twenty-five scholarships a year for five years to high school Tech Prep graduates working toward associate degrees. The local industrial development office included Tech Prep in its promotional efforts in a twelve-page insert entitled "That's Progress," hailing the Richmond County Tech Prep program as an educational pioneer. The implementation of the successful Tech Prep program in Richmond County has depended in large part on a knowledgeable and supportive community. In many ways, future employers have been the key to making the initiative work.

Some of Richmond County's most recent contributions to Tech Prep have been through the operation of the North Carolina Leadership Development Center where they have encouraged the development of Tech Prep programs throughout the state. This center has had the support and willing cooperation of businesses in Richmond County as well as other regions of the state. In cooperation with the North Carolina Leadership Development Center, R.J. Reynolds Tobacco Company, one of North Carolina's largest employers and supporters of Tech Prep, provided four start-up grants ($25,000 each) for newly developing Tech Prep programs in North Carolina.

R.J. Reynolds Tobacco Company has exceeded this contribution through other grants, luncheons, and initiatives throughout the state to encourage the continued development of Tech Prep programs. However, the most recent contribution of R.J. Reynolds Tobacco Company extends beyond North Carolina to serve the needs of Tech Prep programs across the country. In 1993, Don Haver on behalf of R.J. Reynolds Tobacco Company, led and supported the development of a video for recruiting employer involvement in Tech Prep. The company provided more than 2,000 complimentary copies of the video to members of the National Tech Prep Network at their 1993 spring and fall conferences so that Tech Prep consortia in every state could involve businesses in their Tech Prep initiative.

Issue #4: Setting Specifications and Standards

Most educational initiatives are designed by educators, and that is how it should be. But the criteria for what is important—that is, what should be taught—also are usually determined by educators, and that is not necessarily good. Education needs the frequent "reality check" that comes from being linked with the world of work.

This is *not* to say that all education should be job training. Worthwhile education builds good citizens and strengthens communities. It creates artists and appreciation for the arts. It creates scientists and helps us use the sciences. It creates humanists and facilitates use of the humanities. In short, what we learn should help us to live, appreciate, and be responsible in our communities and around the world. But a worthwhile education should *also* prepare students for their future careers. And career-oriented education should be based on specifications from the employers who create and control the jobs.

Developing appropriate specifications requires that a group of eight to fifteen employers who commonly hire workers for similar jobs meet together and collectively agree on what new workers should know and be able to do to enter a specific job and progress in a given career path. The resulting list of job competencies will not contain everything that any one employer would want, but it will contain most of what all of the participating employers want.

In designing a Tech Prep curriculum, as we have seen, it is important for employers to project ahead at least five or six years to describe the skills and competencies they will want in *future* employees, not those they require of current employees. (After all, new Tech Prep students will likely not be full-time workers for four to six years.) This means it is important to involve the business representatives who are in a position to foresee the future of their industry and where it is taking them.

When the competency list has been prepared, it is the educators' job to transform it first into a list of teaching objectives and later into a curriculum aimed at producing those competencies. However, some educators have found that they benefit greatly from having employers work alongside them during the process of curriculum design and development.

But whether or not employers are involved in the development stages, they definitely should be involved in validating the completed curriculum. That is, the same employer group that created the competency list should review the curriculum design and verify that the content does indeed provide the knowledge and skills that the job requires.

A prime example of such a successful partnership between employers and educators has emerged in the Houston, Texas, area. Rockwell International and NASA have been working with three area community colleges and with local school systems to develop a curriculum that prepares Tech Prep students as technicians for the aerospace industry. When the partnership began, Rockwell and NASA provided their own engineers and training personnel to work with the faculty in determining the skills and outcomes needed. A staff person at Rockwell was even assigned full-time to coordinate with the secondary and postsecondary faculty to assure competency and quality.

Three different technician programs have emerged as a result of this employer-educator collaboration: instrumentation and control, microelectronics, and electromechanical. In addition, the close relationship established between the schools and Rockwell is affecting other schools and employers throughout the aerospace industry and in other areas as well.

While the content of these programs assures an aerospace technician trained and prepared for space station operations, for instance, the curriculum leaves other types of occupations open to the student as well. For example, Art Aamoth, the Executive Director of the Houston Business Roundtable and representative for the petrochemical industry, has recommended a review of the Tech Prep aerospace program and noted that there is likely a close relationship between the skills of the aerospace technicians and the skills needed for the technicians in the petrochemical industry.

Because the petrochemical and aerospace industries are among the largest employers in the region, Aamoth along with other employers in these industries is planning for Tech Prep to be the number-one education and training initiative for their future workforce. They have expressed interested in evaluating the common skills across industry lines to develop a pool of technicians in the metropolitan area who could work in either industry.

Issue #5: Assuring Program Quality

Representatives of the businesses, industries, and service organizations who plan to employ future Tech Prep/Associate Degree graduates depend on this program to help them transform their workforce, so they naturally have an interest in assuring the quality of the entire program. They do this in part through their involvement in establishing a need and a policy demand for Tech Prep, recruiting students, providing specifications, and assisting in curriculum design. But ongoing review and assessment is another aspect of quality assurance by employers. In this role, employers should ask:

- Are we recruiting capable students?
- Will they know the job content?
- Will they be able to function effectively in the work environment?
- Can they be retrained if their jobs change?
- Are they capable of advancing in their career?
- Will future changes in job requirements be reflected in revisions and modifications in the Tech Prep program content?

Of course, the final quality-check question will be: "Are the Tech Prep graduates performing satisfactorily on the job?"

The Roanoke Area Tech Prep Consortium in Roanoke, Virginia, has worked through several avenues to assure program quality on an ongoing basis. They began these efforts with a survey taken during the planning stages of the Tech Prep program. Thirty teachers and counselors of all levels and disciplines were hired to work with a group of fifty graduate students at Virginia Technical College to contact almost seven hundred businesses in the area. The participants were trained to conduct personal, on-site visits to each business to find out how the educational community could help the businesses and students' transition into the workplace. The results of this survey varied with the needs of large and small employers; they included characteristics of sought-after employees and ideas for including specific skills and areas of knowledge into local secondary and postsecondary schools.

After the survey was completed, a panel of educational experts evaluated the results and worked more directly with employers to identify specialty career areas in local demand; these included automated manufacturing, international marketing, and early childhood development. In addition, they classified careers into clusters and identified common basic skills needed across all career areas.

Today, with the Roanoke Area Tech Prep program successfully in place, the process of quality assurance continues. Employers still provide two-day orientations for teachers to explain the kind of work their businesses do and the kind of employees they need. Employers also offer internships to students who have strong academic preparation but few technical skills, and many employers serve on advisory councils to review and advise on curriculum, recruitment, and placement.

Most recently, local business representatives have been trying to help the schools incorporate Total Quality Management techniques for empowering their students. They believe that the students are the schools' "frontline workers" and should be involved in every aspect of Tech Prep from curriculum design to promotion of the program.

Issue #6: Providing Resources

In today's dismal school-finance climate, few if any educational programs are receiving budget support beyond the bare necessities. Often, the resources for program enhancement—those elements that can make a difference between a good program and a great one—must come from outside sources. Because Tech Prep is a career-oriented approach to education and because it is designed to meet employer specifications, it is only natural that enhancement resources will be requested from one of the program's significant beneficiaries—the employers.

Many different kinds of employer resources can be provided to Tech Prep consortia. Most of them fall into one of four categories:

- money for planning and faculty development,
- equipment and facilities for laboratories,
- loaned faculty and administrators, and
- worksite learning experiences (for faculty as well as students).

All of these resources can be vital to the ongoing health of the Tech Prep program. However, *how* the resources are provided makes a big difference in how helpful they are. A review of the practice and experiences of previous vocational/technical programs could result in a list of "dos and don'ts" for employer involvement:

- *Do participate actively.* Passive involvement—just allowing the company's name to be used or holding membership on a program advisory committee can be worse than doing nothing at all—because it gives a false impression of true involvement. Agreeing to program objectives and curriculum content that were created by someone else may not ensure that a company will continue to support the program by hiring its graduates.

- *Don't lecture or complain* about how the program doesn't meet your standards; be a part of the process of improving it.

- *Focus the resources invested.* Don't just throw money or equipment at the program. Take the time to assess what will truly improve the program from the employer's view and produce more able graduates.

The relationship of the Boeing Company with the public school systems in Washington provides a positive example of resources provided in an appropriate manner. Despite the fact that the Boeing Company remains the number-one commercial aircraft company in the world and the number-one exporter in the United States, the company faces some major obstacles, both internal and external. Computer-aided design, robotics, numerically controlled machines, and the general use of computers are just a few of the changing technical skills that employees need in order for the company to remain competitive.

Because of these needs, the Boeing Company has been committed to the Tech Prep initiative in Washington. Since 1989, Boeing has provided more than three million dollars to the Tech Prep initiative. These resources have been used for the teaching of applied academics in twenty-one school districts throughout the state and providing support for the articulation of math and science courses with the community college curriculum.

In addition to providing dollars, the Boeing Company invites math and science teachers in the summer to spend six weeks in the manufacturing environments and learn how employees use the academic skills they are teaching in the classroom. Boeing executives have also served on the special state legislative task force concerned with the acceptance of applied academics as fulfilling university entrance requirements. Their involvement and commitment with the legislature and the Higher Education Coordinating Board played a large part in the ultimate approval of these courses.

*   *   *   *   *

The strong partnership in Geneva, Illinois, among WMX Technologies Inc., seven public school districts, and Waubonsee Community College provides another example of active involvement by employers and the focused use of corporate resources. The first project after the partnership was formed was to implement an enhanced Principles of Technology course for high school Tech Prep students. The course was to be housed and operated at the corporate site, where many of WMX Technologies' research labs are located. With the endorsement of the parent company CEO, a teaching facility was designed and built among the other advanced-technology labs. WMX Technologies Inc. provided safety equipment, office space for the instructor, a computer and software, and all necessary lab equipment. WMX Technologies also considers the Principles of Technology teacher of Batavia Public Schools as an "adopted" company employee.

Since the Principles of Technology lab opened, approximately thirty-five employees from WMX Technologies Inc. volunteer their time to give class demonstrations, assist with laboratory experiments, and provide tutoring

*when needed. In addition, these volunteers serve as coaches and consultants in
the annual regional science contests.*

Both Boeing and WMX Technologies employees are committed to the
Tech Prep initiative and are focusing their resources to help in the programs
and curriculum because they truly believe their efforts will ultimately
develop a strong workforce. Their continuing and progressively increased
support over a period of several years testifies to an active involvement that
goes far beyond donations of material resources and membership on
advisory boards. In return, they not only have the satisfaction of knowing
that their contributions are truly making a difference in the quality of new
workers coming from the Tech Prep programs; they also stand to benefit
directly from including these new workers on their payrolls.

Issue #7: Mentoring Tech Prep Students[1]

It has been said that *you can't prepare today's students for tomorrow's world
using yesterday's methods.* However, some of yesterday's methods are just
what today's students need. And a mentoring program—an organized
system of pairing a Tech Prep student with an adult who is working in the
student's chosen field—is a case in point.

Ostensibly, Tech Prep mentoring exists for students; it helps them make a
smooth transition from school to the world of work. And students do benefit
immensely from a well-run mentoring program. In the first place, a
mentoring program has holding power for students; it provides them with
incentives to stay in school and in the Tech Prep program itself. A number of
factors—the rigor of the curriculum, the need to earn money, and the lure of
time-shortened options—can tempt students to leave Tech Prep programs.
But mentors, by extending the students' support system and clearly showing
them the application of what they are learning, can help keep students
focused beyond the limited scope of next weekend or next month and
toward the goal of completing the program. In addition, by exposing
students to a wide variety of jobs and job situations, mentoring helps
students decide ahead of time whether their chosen career path is really
suitable for them.

But students aren't the only ones who benefit from a mentoring program;
the benefits extend to the educational institutions as well. For example,
retention of students in a Tech Prep program helps it grow quickly and
develop a track record, and this in turn attracts other students. In addition,
the contact with industry personnel helps keep both teachers and curricula

---

1. This section was excerpted and adapted from Maggie Rice, "Developing an Effective
   Mentoring Program" in Dan Hull and Dale Parnell, *Tech Prep/Associate Degree: A Win/Win
   Experience* (Waco, TX: Center for Occupational Research and Development, 1991), 287–98.

up-to-date, and the employers' commitment to the Tech Prep students who will be the workers of tomorrow also helps strengthen those employers' commitment to Tech Prep education today. Finally, mentoring programs eventually benefit themselves: today's protégés are very likely to become tomorrow's mentors.

Employers, too, benefit from a well-run mentoring program. Graduates of mentoring programs are likely to be well-trained and highly motivated job applicants—just the kind of employees businesses and industries want and need. And employers save time and money hiring Tech Prep graduates who have benefited from a mentoring program—not only because they require less training and orientation, but also because the mentoring process gives employers a chance to prescreen potential employees. Employers have a better idea of what they're getting because they've known these kids since high school.

The Tech Prep program run by Leander Independent School District and Austin Community College in Austin, Texas, sponsors mentoring activities for each Tech Prep student from the beginning of the sophomore year through the completion of the associate degree. During the grade in which most Tech Prep students make a decision about the career cluster or major of studies that they will pursue, the students take a career/interest inventory. Parents are brought into the decision-making process, and each student is counseled individually. During this preparatory year, new students are "adopted" by their first mentors—high school seniors who are already in the program.

At the beginning of the Tech Prep students' eleventh-grade school year, they attend a back-to-school party to meet their already selected adult mentors. Throughout this year and the rest of the program, the mentors reinforce the importance of learning basic academics and other important curricula as well as help the student make connections between their academic competencies and the work they will be expected to do on the job.

When enrolled in their postsecondary program, the Tech Prep program students work with their mentors in designing an action plan for the rest of their time in the Tech Prep program. Mentors also serve as adjunct faculty and resource persons during the tenure of the program. During the summers, the teachers participate in "shadowing" at the worksites (observing what employees do during a typical work day), while the students complete summer projects at the worksite. During the senior year, students visit worksites and interview various employees who are on the job.

Once the students graduate from the community college, the mentors show their support by attending a spring banquet. At this time those students who have obtained employment or plan to continue their education at a university are recognized. Every student is affirmed in some way for his or her perseverance in seeing the Tech Prep program through to completion. And although the mentoring program features no guarantee of employment, it stands to reason that mentored students would then have an edge in finding a job.

Issue #8: Providing a Worksite Learning Component

- What encourages "at-risk" students to be interested and enthusiastic about their education?

- How do you motivate fifteen-to-nineteen-year-old students to continue their 4+2 curriculum beyond high school?

- How do students confirm that their career choices are good ones?

- How do you train students in job-specific skills on modern, expensive equipment?

- How do you teach students about problem-solving, working in teams, climate and quality standards of the workplace, attitudes and interpersonal skills required by employers?

- What is an effective way for students to prepare for and make the transition into the workplace?

The answer to all these questions may be a good worksite learning program offered as part of a Tech Prep education.

Few would argue that the best employee is one who has a good academic and technical background plus a certain amount of practical experience. Sound academic preparation provides the foundation for most technical education and training and offers students the flexibility of later changing careers or specialty areas. But both high school and college graduates who have acquired *only* academic skills often find that their lack of worksite experience is a substantial obstacle in obtaining a jobs. (This is true in both the manufacturing and the service sector.)

Tech Prep program developers would do well to examine reports from employer-based groups that identify their needs for new skills in the American workplace. Many of the "new skills" can of course be learned in appropriate classrooms and laboratories that are using new curricula and better teaching methods. However, many of these skills—quality, productivity, timeliness, and team approaches to problem-solving—can be strengthened, and certain other skills requiring the work environment and equipment can be learned best if Tech Prep students are actually engaged in jobs related to their intended careers.

The German apprenticeship model, which has been very successful in Europe and which puts students to work at an early age in the profession they have chosen, offers some useful ideas on how the blending between education and experience might be structured into an educational system.[2] It is unrealistic, however, to believe that the German apprenticeship model could, or even should, be copied in the United States. Americans tend to balk at the idea of locking students into a specific vocation at an early age, which appears to happen in the German system. They fear that such practical training almost inevitably skimps on academic preparation, thus turning out graduates who are prepared to do only one thing.

These are valid fears and certainly should be addressed in setting up a worksite learning system. Nevertheless, the basic idea of on-the-job learning is a valuable one that can be adopted and used very effectively in a Tech Prep program—whether the arrangements between employers and students involve apprenticeships, cooperative programs, or work-study programs.

Listed below are some guidelines that employers and educators might consider when working to include worksite learning in a Tech Prep/Associate Degree program:

- *Employers and educators should agree on the purpose of the worksite learning program.* This will mean ongoing discussion about the expectations and the needs of all parties concerned. The most effective worksite learning programs are based on the agreement that the students should learn from mutually supportive activities in the classroom and workplace—that Tech Prep programs should combine academic classroom work with current job practices and procedures.

- *Employers and educators should arrive at a consensus about learning objectives.* A representative committee in each career cluster should discuss, identify, specify, and measure what the students need to learn, both in the classroom and in the workplace. This discussion should provide an opportunity for both employers and educators to identify job-market needs and make projections.

- *A reasonable and progressive schedule for worksite learning should be drawn up.* Work programs can begin as early as the ninth or tenth grade. In those early years, however, a student should work no more than eight hours per week. In the later high school years (grades eleven and twelve), a student could work up to but not more than fifteen hours per week. Full-time worksite learning during student vacation periods should be aimed at achieving objectives that cannot be covered during the regular school year.

---

2. Stephen Hamilton, *Apprenticeship for Adulthood: Preparing Youth for the Future* (New York, NY: The Free Press, A Division of Macmillan, Inc., 1990).

- *Worksite learning should not be confused with student-aid programs or cheap labor for firms.* The worksite learning experience must involve interested people at the site, willing to invest time and effort in the progress of the student. Too often, students are "dumped" at the site and left there to do "menial" busy work.

- *There should be signed agreements between the student and the employer who provides the worksite learning environment.* A formal agreement helps reinforce the employer's investment in the program and makes sure the student is informed about employer expectations and program objectives.

- *Appropriate credit should be given for demonstrated competencies obtained through worksite experiences.* After students have begun work, both employers and educators must come to an agreement on what level of competency the student is expected to achieve and how that competency is to be tested. Credit should be awarded by both school and employer.

- *Expectations for the program should be focused appropriately.* Students' expectations should be based on career preparation, interest, and ability. Employers' expectations should be based on how their efforts will contribute to a better workforce. Educators' expectations should be based on the ways that practical work experience can reinforce academic learning.

Worksite learning can be a meaningful part of Tech Prep curricula throughout the life of the program. When designing a worksite learning component as part of the Tech Prep process, many Tech Prep consortia have found it helpful to begin by determining broad outcomes for student achievement in each of the three major phases: grades nine and ten, grades eleven and twelve, and the two postsecondary years of the program. With these outcomes in mind, it is easier to determine which ones can best be achieved in a school-based learning environment and which could be enhanced through a worksite learning environment. Figure 1 represents such a process.

Many of the worksite activities that are emerging in Tech Prep/Associate Degree programs are forming as part of a new initiative called Youth Apprenticeship. Youth Apprenticeship programs that are being tested in the United States were started as early as 1990 in some cases and have drawn ideas from studies of the German system. The primary impetus for Youth Apprenticeship, however, is the need for all students to be better prepared for employment through learning that integrates academic and technical instruction with guided practical experiences in the workplace.

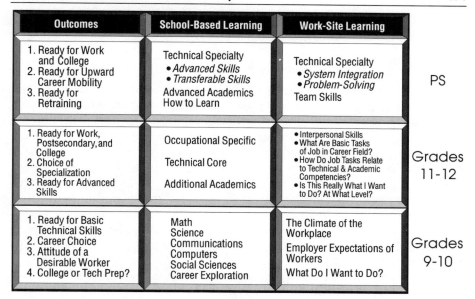

Outcomes	School-Based Learning	Work-Site Learning	
1. Ready for Work and College 2. Ready for Upward Career Mobility 3. Ready for Retraining	Technical Specialty • *Advanced Skills* • *Transferable Skills* Advanced Academics How to Learn	Technical Specialty • *System Integration* • *Problem-Solving* Team Skills	PS
1. Ready for Work, Postsecondary, and College 2. Choice of Specialization 3. Ready for Advanced Skills	Occupational Specific Technical Core Additional Academics	• Interpersonal Skills • What Are Basic Tasks of Job in Career Field? • How Do Job Tasks Relate to Technical & Academic Competencies? • Is This Really What I Want to Do? At What Level?	Grades 11-12
1. Ready for Basic Technical Skills 2. Career Choice 3. Attitude of a Desirable Worker 4. College or Tech Prep?	Math Science Communications Computers Social Sciences Career Exploration	The Climate of the Workplace Employer Expectations of Workers What Do I Want to Do?	Grades 9-10

Figure 1. Structure and Purpose of a Tech Prep Curriculum

Youth Apprenticeship has been defined by proposed legislation and other supporting organizations as an employer/school partnership, preceded by career exploration, that includes integrated academic instruction, structured job training, and paid worksite experience. It is offered to students beginning in the eleventh grade or twelfth grade and results in receipt of a high school diploma and receipt of an approved certificate of mastery (if appropriate), entry into a postsecondary program, or permanent employment.

The West Virginia model for youth apprenticeship is one of five national models sponsored by the Council of Chief State School Officers (CCSS). This program systematically connects youth apprenticeship with higher education as an option within the Tech Prep/Associate Degree program.

The nationally registered West Virginia program accepts students in the second semester of their junior year of high school, during which time a final assessment and screening are accomplished. These students then spend the summer prior to their senior year as employed apprentices at a particular worksite under the oversight of a Diversified Co-op Coordinator, who provides both pre-employment counseling and worksite supervision.

After the summer, Tech Prep students who choose the Youth Apprenticeship option will spend up to 40 percent of their senior year on the job, while spending the remaining 60 percent on their school-based studies. Graduating seniors who have participated in this program may then enter an associate-degree program with up to forty-three hours of credit through a separate agreement between the Bureau of Apprenticeship and Training and West Virginia community colleges.

Issue #9: Overcoming Resistance to Change

Businesses have changed over the past eight to ten years; at least, they have changed the way they do business. During that time, most United States businesses have realized that their greatest competitor is not the business next door or in the next town or even in the next state, but the businesses overseas. They have been confronted with the fact that they can't compete globally by using low-skill, low-wage U.S. workers in the United States. If they want to stay competitive, they must either move their plants out of the country (as some have done) or restructure to become more "lean and mean."

This second approach involves retooling, reorganizing, and sometimes restaffing. It calls for employees who are both highly trained and flexible enough to retrain when necessary. And Tech Prep can provide the new workers needed to take this new, competitive approach—if employers will fully participate in the educational process.

But employers as well as educators sometimes prove resistant to the changes Tech Prep brings. This resistance typically takes one of several forms:

- *Tech Prep requires employers to become far more committed to and involved in the education process than they have ever done.* They are being asked to take a more proactive role in defining needs, designing curricula, and evaluating success. Moreover, they are being asked to participate actively in the educational process, not just look on as interested observers or give their stamp of approval or disapproval. Worksite learning experiences and employee/student mentoring are two examples of this new, proactive role. Employers are sometimes reluctant to assume this new role, just as educators are reluctant to have them included.

- *This newer, proactive commitment will require the time of business/industry's more productive people.* As we have seen, a successful Tech Prep partnership depends on the participation of key policymakers who have a grasp of future needs, not just "expendable" staff who can help with education as a public-relations gesture. Some businesses are reluctant to commit their key employees' time in this way.

- *Tech Prep will cost businesses money,* whether it's a matter of providing release time of highly productive employees, providing financial or material resources, or opening up the workplace as a learning environment. Many businesses are reluctant to spend before-tax profits on new initiatives whose payoff lies somewhere in the future.

- *Not every employer has gotten the message about the new marketplace.* Some are still reluctant to restructure their workplace to incorporate the kind of high-skills, high-wage jobs for which Tech Prep is preparing students. When the report *America's Choice: High Skills or Low Wages*[3] was released in June of 1991, the research estimated that only 5 to 10 percent of all employers had seen the need and restructured. Since that time, however, the number has more than doubled, and this growth trend likely will continue.

On the whole, however, employers are facing the tough choices and paying the price in order to reap the benefits of Tech Prep. Let us hope that educators will do the same.

For Tech Prep to accomplish what is needed in our country:

- to provide a more competent, flexible, empowered workforce;
- to provide a whole range of new and better workers for America's employers; and
- to allow business to grow and create new jobs;

we have to create an entirely new culture among schools and businesses, where both are contributing in mutually supportive ways to provide students with the knowledge and skills that employers need.

Employers are already complaining, advising, encouraging, and spending substantial resources for more education and training that relates to their job needs. But in most instances, it hasn't been very effective, because:

1. Employers are still "standing on the sideline" watching education happen with our young people instead of becoming "education partners" in delivering the curriculum.

2. We haven't sorted out who and where (school vs. worksite) elements of the curriculum can best be taught—or reinforced. Educators and employers must reach a consensus for their mutually supportive roles in educational delivery to allow each to contribute what they can do best.

When these two issues are thoughtfully considered and remedied, we shall have achieved school-work integration which will be a win-win-win experience for educators, employers and students. Tech Prep can be the vehicle to accomplish school-work integration. It's already working in a few sties; it needs to work in a lot more places.

---

3. Commission on the Skills of the American Workforce, *America's Choice: High Skills or Low Wages* (Rochester, NY: National Center on Education and the Economy, 1990).

9.

OPENING MINDS

Making Positive Change a Reality in Our Educational Systems [1]

OPENING DOORS

It is inappropriate to say that change is needed in education today. A more accurate statement might be that change *is occurring* in education today. The issue for parents, educators, employers, policymakers, taxpayers—all who have a stake in the effectiveness of American education—then becomes: *How can we manage change in order to maximize the moment and guarantee positive results?*

Two kinds of change are often seen in the educational environment. The first and most common is *piecemeal change,* which involves tinkering with or modifying the existing structure to make it better. This kind of change can be appropriate and effective when the underlying system is functioning properly and doing what it needs to do.

The second kind of change is *systemic change,* which involves rethinking (making a paradigm shift) and replacing the entire structure of an organization or institution. This kind of change in education is:

- *comprehensive*, applying to every aspect of the educational system;

- *complete*, pervading all levels of the organization, including classroom, district, community, state government, federal government, and industry; and

- *correlative*, relating to learning experiences, administrative support, government funding, and industry/business application.

---

1. The organization, substance, and the original draft for this chapter were contributed by Dr. William Halbert, Vice President for Curriculum Programs at the Center for Occupational Research and Development.

Not surprisingly, change of this sort can be difficult to implement, and it carries a greater risk of failure. Yet this kind of change, when approached with vision and integrity, stands by far the greatest chance of effecting long-term improvement. This is the kind of change that must happen if Tech Prep/Associate Degree is to reach its full potential as an educational reform.

Perhaps the most troubling issue for those looking at this kind of change is the simple fact that no one can be assured of its outcome. Leaders are quick to talk about the problems—what we don't want education to be—but slow in providing workable solutions. A perfect environment for education has yet to be defined or modeled.

Nevertheless, the case for changing our current educational system is clear and strong. During the last century our society has undergone a major shift from an agrarian base to an industrial and then an information base. Transportation has moved from horse to train to car to jet to space shuttle. The dominant form of business has moved from family to bureaucracy to team, and education has moved from the one-room schoolhouse to the current system to whatever lies ahead. And the Tech Prep response, while perhaps just a beginning, may well be the best educational answer so far to this major paradigm shift—the key to moving us where we need to be in decades to come.

Is Change Really Needed?

Although change is inevitable in any system, including the educational system, there is little point in making changes just for changes' sake. The kind of far-reaching, systemic change represented by Tech Prep must be based on a clear sense that such a change is indeed necessary. Obviously, I believe that need does exist in most communities of our nation, and I spell out this need in some detail in the earlier chapters of this book. But to confirm whether a local system really needs to change, I suggest asking the following questions before jumping into reform.

- Are local schools, industry, and community doing a satisfactory job of working together to prepare the majority of students for their future?

- Do the majority of students in secondary and postsecondary institutions appreciate their education while in school, and are they satisfied with their education after they graduate?

- Are there clear opportunities in the community for high school graduates to enter postsecondary schools and training programs? How smooth a transition can they make?

- Are graduating students adequately prepared to enter the workforce of the twenty-first century?

- Do schools target the needs of the majority of students with the most effective and proven teaching/learning approaches to date?

- Do students have knowledge of various types of careers and have clear pathways they can pursue to achieve them?

- Is there a forum in the community for discussing and resolving issues like these regarding education and change?

The answers to these questions will not necessarily propel schools or communities or people into change, but will urge schools and communities and people to consider the consequences of *not* making change.

What Are the Goals of Change?

A second factor that must be taken into account when considering any kind of change is *what the change is intended to accomplish*—in other words, the *goals* of change. Asking this question can be extremely helpful in determining what kinds of specific changes will be necessary to achieve those goals, and this in turn will help ensure that change is meaningful and effective. (Again, the idea is not to bring about change for change's sake, but to enact the kind of systemic change that truly makes a positive difference.)

In January 1993, a group of project directors from fifteen of the model Tech Prep consortia in the United States met to discuss, among other issues, this vital question of change in our educational system. The first concern had to do with goals: "What do we expect Tech Prep to accomplish?"

The goal that received the greatest affirmation from the project directors was that of *raising students' academic and technological skills*. One approach to reaching this goal is to reduce the number of students enrolled in the general studies program and to make sure that most, if not all, students are enrolled in a more specific program of studies (such as Tech Prep or college prep) that encourages students to complete higher levels of curriculum.

Another strategy for achieving the first goal is to move from compartmentalized education toward horizontally and vertically integrated education as explained in chapter 5 and to move toward school-work integration as described in chapter 8. An integrated approach may require both academic and vocational educators to adopt new attitudes and methods, but it promises to create more connections and avenues for understanding the curriculum and give students a more meaningful, complete perspective on life and work.

A second goal that the Tech Prep consortium group identified was *increasing the number and percentage of students enrolling in and completing postsecondary training*. Accomplishing this goal may require a change of attitude on the part of educators, parents, and students about what "postsecondary" means and the opportunities that an associate degree can offer students. A baccalaureate degree is not the only—or even the best—route to a "college education" or a good job.

More important, however, working toward this goal will require breaking down the walls between secondary and postsecondary institutions to create more avenues for communication and collaboration. Many secondary educators have never been on their local community college campus, do not know the types of programs that the college offers, and have never considered the overlaps and gaps between the courses that are taught in high school and the courses that are taught at the community college.

A third goal considered by the Tech Prep group was *developing a world-class educational program for the majority of students*. The achievement of such a goal would be evidenced by student outcomes that include employability as well as cognitive and psychomotor skills. Reaching this goal would require changing the attitudes and perceptions of educators, parents, and students about how excellence in education is defined. Students who do not go on to university studies can still receive a first-class education and can do so through Tech Prep/Associate Degree.

A fourth desired goal identified by the Tech Prep group was *preparing graduates of high school and postsecondary programs for employment flexibility and for lifelong learning*. This would lead to better-prepared students and an improved workforce, which in turn would result in a better quality of life, a stronger nation and ultimately a more competitive global economy. Achieving such an objective would clearly require designing and developing a flexible program that offers opportunities, avenues, and useful skills and knowledge—a program that does not lock students into a track or a dead-end program. The curriculum content, instruction methods, and guidance system would need to concentrate on giving students the skills they need to keep on learning, even after they have finished the basic program.

In addition to these four goals identified by the Tech Prep group, I would add a fifth: *teaching students the way they learn*. The findings of cognitive science that we review in chapter 3 suggest that different people process information and acquire skills in different ways. Providing an effective education for all students would therefore require a consideration of these differences in learning styles and an adoption of teaching and assessment methods that take these differences into consideration. Because the majority of schools are geared toward one particular learning style (the one employed by a minority of students), achieving this objective will involve changing attitudes, teaching styles, and organizational structures of a school system.

The Human Factor

Not surprisingly, all the desired outcomes listed above are outcomes that Tech Prep addresses directly, and the changes needed to bring about these outcomes are the very changes that a successful Tech Prep program will require. Whom exactly will these changes affect—and who will be involved in making the changes? This question introduces another important factor of change: people. Unless the human factor is taken into account, a change initiative has little chance of success.

Most obviously, a change to Tech Prep would most directly affect students, teachers, administrators, and employers (business and industry leaders). But parents, counselors, politicians, government officials, community leaders, and taxpayers will feel the ripples of change as well. Can anyone be isolated from the issue of improved schools, prepared students, and job availability?

Recently I ran across a game entitled "Making Change for School Improvement."[2] It is intended for use by business managers and employers who are anticipating change and want to see how their employees might react. The creator of the game refers to five "adopter personalities" to demonstrate how people differ in their readiness to accept change. These adopter types as identified by the game include:

- *innovators,* who are eager to try new ideas,

- *leaders,* who are open to change but more thoughtful,

- *early majority,* who are cautious but deliberate,

- *late majority,* who tend to be skeptical of new ideas and intransigent, and

- *resisters,* who tend to be suspicious of and generally opposed to new ideas.

By the completion of the game, it becomes very clear to the players that the basic personality of people involved in change may be as important to the outcome as the issue or circumstances surrounding change. The clear implication for the beginning of a Tech Prep initiative is that all these different personalities must be taken into account in the process of making change stick.

---

2. Available from The Network, Inc., 300 Brickstone Square, Suite 900, Andover, MA 01810.

The Barriers to Change

Any change that affects such a large group of people—even a positive change—is bound to encounter resistance (especially from some of the "adopter personalities" mentioned above!). The following list, which was brainstormed by the same group of Tech Prep project directors that outlined the desired outcomes, points to some of the common issues that often stand in the way of productive change—and that often serve as barriers to the implementation of Tech Prep.

protection of "turf"	lack of direction
state requirements	loss of jobs
red tape	stereotypes
lack of a sense of ownership	performance review
prejudice	adverse publicity
outdated evaluation system	age of participants
lack of parental involvement	limited resources
differing philosophical perspectives	distractions
inaccurate perception of student success	government restrictions
	long-standing tradition
changing values	purists
labor unions	elitism
politics	limited staff development
changing roles	competition for resources
organizational structure	inappropriate physical settings
tenure	fixed attitudes about school
lack of knowledge	teacher biases
history and tradition	fear of new technologies
schedules	fear of change
lack of understanding	leaders under stress
too many experts	class size
fear of loss of control	too many priorities
confusion of terms	hidden agendas
cultural differences	"This too shall pass"
need to maintain the system	

It should be clear that most of these barriers are "people issues" as well, and most of them stem from a very basic human emotion: fear. Many stem from fear of the unknown: "What if we fail?" "What if we succeed, then what?" Other barriers involve the fear of loss: loss of privacy, loss of control, loss of identity, loss of familiarity, loss of direction, loss of security. Many of these fears are wrapped up in a comfort zone. Even though people may be in pain, they are at least familiar with that pain and therefore sometimes unwilling to do what is necessary to relieve that pain.

These are common human responses to change of any sort. They are real and they can be formidable. But they can be overcome if change is approached in the right way. The keys to moving people out of their fears are communication, guidance, motivation, and leadership.

To Change or Not to Change: Confronting the Myths

Some of the most powerful barriers to change are myths about change that have become established in the popular imagination. One of the keys to effecting positive change, therefore, is to debunk some of these myths, such as:

- *"People don't ever change."* Ask yourself if you still think, feel, dress, talk, walk, play, work, love, operate in exactly the same way you did twenty years ago, or ten, or five, or perhaps even yesterday. That should be enough to convince you that people *do* change in their thoughts, feelings, and behaviors. On occasion, because of major happenings in our lives (the loss of a loved one, illness or injury, a financial reversal or windfall), changes occur quickly. More often, the change is gradual or even imperceptible.

- *"People always resist change."* The truth of this statement is that people resist *being changed* far more than they resist the change itself. A large population enjoys shopping, but hates to be sold. When one has influence or control in the change, that change can be a motivating factor in one's life. It is when that control is taken away and manipulation becomes the order of the day that resistance raises its head. One of a human being's greatest needs is to remain autonomous.

- *"You can't teach an old dog new tricks."* It is true that the older human beings become, the more they tend to resist change just for changes' sake. But this doesn't mean adults can't change; it just means they are more likely to pick their changes carefully and selectively. They are more prone to ask *why* before jumping into a change. When presented with a compelling rationale, they are just as likely to embrace positive change such as Tech Prep and support it enthusiastically.

Principles of Effective Change

Having explored some of the important dynamics of change, including the need for change, the desired outcomes, the human factors involved, and the various barriers that may stand in the way of change, it might be appropriate to outline some basic principles for effecting real and lasting change of any sort. An awareness of these principles can make a significant difference in the success of any local Tech Prep venture:

Principle #1: Effective Change Requires Clear Objectives.

Keeping the focus clear reduces the effect of resistance, interruptions, and other problems on the expected outcome. Ideally, the primary objectives for a local Tech Prep initiative would be based on the input of all concerned parties and would be spelled out in a policy statement at the beginning of the push for acceptance.

What are appropriate objectives for a Tech Prep initiative? To be successful, a local Tech Prep effort needs:

- Broad support from the school and community,

- Enthusiastic approval by educational leaders,

- Staff development at all stages of the change initiative, and

- Institutionalization—moving the reform into the curriculum, classroom, budget, school policy, and pupil acceptance.

Principle #2: Effective Change Has a People Focus.

People make change happen—not organizations, institutions, or groups. If the help and support of individuals is sought first, the institutions they represent will be included in the change action. The time that is taken to enlist and educate implementers carefully at the beginning of an initiative will pay dividends as the process continues.

It's helpful to remember that every individual involved in a particular reform has certain needs that he or she hopes to fill. Understanding this basic "What's in it for me?" motivation greatly increases the likelihood of involving the necessary people in the desired reform.

To enhance the people focus, a social setting may be the best environment for meeting and discussing future directions. One Tech Prep seminar leader said, "We always include food whenever we have a meeting. On one occasion we did not provide the food, and the next meeting was poorly attended."

Principle #3: Effective Change Is Inclusive.

The people who will be primarily affected by change and particularly those who will be responsible for carrying it out are often the same individuals who should become part of each step of the change itself. It is highly ineffective to present a major reform to someone as a "done deal" and expect consent or approval. When implementers are involved they become stakeholders in the project; their own identity becomes a part of the drive to bring about change.

It is critical to include as many players as possible—teachers, counselors, administrators, staff persons, parents, and representatives of business and industry—in the planning meetings and other change arenas. A policy of inclusion will ensure that the power and influence needed to win acceptance of the program are balanced with the technical skills and support necessary to pull it off. Some people are better at thinking up ideas, and other people are better at carrying them out. Recognition can be given to all for their contribution and accomplishment. One Tech Prep leader made creative use of this principle by pinpointing the person who would probably offer the greatest resistance to the reform movement and deliberately giving that individual some responsibility. In this way, the leader was able to redirect a potential negative response into a positive output.

Principle #4: Effective Change Is a Process.

The success of a Tech Prep initiative rarely hinges on a single yes or no vote, a single meeting, a single course. Instead, each step becomes another move in the right direction. The process is just as important as the goal itself. Processes can be modified, altered, embellished, enlarged, and adapted to local conditions. Consequently each Tech Program will be shaped by the processes of its implementation. This is healthy, because it keeps the initiative flexible and responsive to the needs of the community.

Principle #5: Effective Change Takes Time.

Systemic change of the sort represented by Tech Prep/Associate Degree will not happen overnight. It takes time for participants to get used to the idea, to be convinced of its benefits, to consider how the basic principles of Tech Prep reform can be applied in a specific local situation. It also takes time to develop working relationships between key players, to develop procedures for attracting students into the program, and to test the procedures on small groups before committing to a full-scale program. For all these reasons, Tech Prep/Associate Degree is not a quick-fix solution. In fact, as we will see, rushing the process of implementation is one of the best ways to ensure its failure.

Principle #6: Effective Change Requires a Bifocal View.

Because systemic change does take a while to implement, it's important to keep an eye on both the long-term objectives and the short-term tasks. For instance, the long-term objective for Tech Prep is to bring about educational reform that provides improved opportunity for students, and an upgraded workforce for employers, but the short-term issue may be today's meeting. A bifocal view of a Tech Prep initiative insists upon the balance between present and future demands.

Principle #7: Effective Change Is Based on a Higher Calling.

For long-term improvement to be realized, the instigators of change need to be motivated by more than just self-interest. ("What's in it for me?" can be a powerful motivator, but it rarely has the staying power to push a new initiative through to completion.) For Tech Prep/Associate Degree to be all it can be, we must place the students' welfare above parental expectations, teacher security, administrative turf protection, board members' fear of potential repercussions, and employers' desire for cheap workers.

Principle #8: Effective Change Requires Effective Communication.

More specifically, this means using simple, direct language and a commitment to maintaining clear understanding among the various participants. Someone has said that the mark of an educated person is the ability to take a complicated idea and make it simple. If educators are not careful, however, Tech Prep has the potential to become a bureaucratic quagmire of steps, stages, methods, slogans, and otherwise confusing rhetoric that eventually leads to confusion and poor response. Acronyms and terminology may not be familiar to all and may keep the message from being heard by everyone. Useful language is that which is common to most citizens—educators, employers, parents, and politicians. There is little to be accomplished by a wordsmith vocabulary or by "insider" language.

Helping Change to Happen ("Selling Tech Prep")

Whatever the application and whatever the goal, the basic process of bringing about change—in effect, helping change to happen—is the same. Human beings require a movement of thought from *what is* to *what might be* by going through certain definitive stages, and the process of influencing change must follow the same step-by-step process. The intensity of each stage and what it entails depend of course upon many factors. Changes that affect physiological needs are often quickly processed, while changes that are philosophical and psychological can take a longer time. The value of the change to the participant often determines the speed at which the stages are handled.

Stage #1: An Awareness That a New Idea Exists

This generic insight is usually broad-based, ill-defined, and loosely presented. It may come in the form of a promised benefit or proffered hope ("Tomorrow will be a better day!"), but at this point individuals will not need much clarity as to where, when, or how that hope will come. The primary appeal at this point is to the emotions, and the presentation is geared to the motivational needs of an individual. "I feel good about this idea and I feel like it will be good news for me and others."

As far as Tech Prep is concerned, this first stage might be handled by communicating that Tech Prep exists and that it is a new way of working with students to help them become more successful. In addition, some of the following benefits might be listed:

- encouraging students in new ways of learning that have relevance and meaning,

- eliminating the general track that leads to nowhere,

- offering a real future after high school—higher education and a real-world career,

- elevating classroom productivity due to increased attendance and decreased dropouts,

- integrating secondary and postsecondary educational pursuits to eliminate unnecessary delays and duplications, and

- accomplishing national goals for a better-trained workforce.

Stage #2: Education

This stage provides the participant an opportunity to know the facts. The primary appeal at this point is to the mind. The data itself is motivating and gives the participant the information needed to reason, problem-solve, and conjecture about the future. The facts tell me that something has happened and that something can be proven.

At stage two, for instance, a Tech Prep initiative might be presented by listing some facts and figures that show how Tech Prep is changing the face of American education. For instance:

- At Rhode Island Community College (Providence, Lincoln, and Warwick branches), retention of students entering postsecondary education has risen to a record 78 percent.

- At Norfolk Public Schools in Virginia, scores on the state-mandated TAP tests for eleventh-graders have increased annually since 1988, the year Tech Prep was initiated.

- In Swansea, South Carolina, the dropout rate moved from 7.7 percent (highest in South Carolina) to 1.03 percent after two years of Tech Prep. Over the same period, percentages of high school students entering postsecondary education increased from 35 percent to 52 percent.

- At Roanoke, Virginia, the dropout rate decreased from 4.8 percent in 1990 to 1.8 percent in 1992.

Stage #3: Testing or Trial

This stage is significant for anyone looking at a major change. The testing stage is a contrived experience that features limited use of an idea in a relatively safe setting. Such an experience gives participants an opportunity to put a toe in the water without having to buy a boat.

Stage three can be managed in a Tech Prep setting by initiating a pilot class or program. Rather than turning an entire school system upside-down, a certain section of the school program can be identified as an isolated model for trial and error.

Many Tech Prep consortia have elected to pilot their new curricula with a voluntary group of students in one high school during the first year. This gives teachers an opportunity to get comfortable with the new approach to instruction and administrators time to recognize and deal with any potential problems in setting up classrooms and counseling students through the program.

Still another way for a new Tech Prep consortium to get a toe in the Tech Prep water is to "go to school" on successful TPAD programs. The experiences of other Tech Prep consortia can be a valuable source of information and ideas about what works and what doesn't.

Stage #4: Commitment

A commitment to comprehensive change of this nature does not occur without a strong foundation; this stage builds upon stages one, two, and three. To expect people to commit to a reform without appropriate awareness, education, and trial is like expecting a flower to grow with no sunshine, water, or soil.

Tech Prep leaders must realize that a change of this type requires long-term planning and strategic thinking. A quick-fix approach to education will simply wave another trendy flag in the faces of already fatigued followers. Commitment requires a buy-in from participants—educators, employers, and students alike—that comes from personal processing and individual accountability.

Troubleshooting Change

Not every attempt at deep-seated, systemic change will succeed. Not every Tech Prep program that is planned becomes fully established. A look at what sometimes goes wrong can be instructive. Why do attempts at change sometimes fail?

- The participants might not be ready for change—either because the initiative proceeded too quickly or because the time was simply not right.

- Unclear driving forces or unclear vision may sabotage the plans. Mixed motives or murky ideas can put any initiative on the road to nowhere.

- The lack of an effective master plan or strategy to guide the implementers can leave everyone floundering.

- Those in charge of implementing change may fail to exert decisive or authoritative leadership.

- Poor communication or lack of progress reporting during the transition may cause participants to lose their sense of direction.

- An unclear or inadequate problem-solving mechanism may lead to circular arguments, endless meetings, and ongoing grudges among participants.

- Failure to eliminate busywork may keep the vital work from being done.

- Weak incentives for participation in change may cause motivation to drop.

- Inadequate training of faculty or staff may result in poor-quality work as well as hindering the process of teacher buy-in.

- Participants may feel they are being forced to change instead of participating in change.

- Poor follow-up on promises made can stall motivation.

- Participants may feel that change threatens their jobs and may wonder how they fit into the new structure.

All of these possibilities exist in any change endeavor, even those with the best of planning and the highest level of commitment. It is possible to be moving along smoothly with a new endeavor and then find that one concern may be breaking down communication, motivation, cooperation, decision-making or some other dynamic. It is more probable, however, that a number of breakdowns are occurring and that a complete and systematic survey will be needed to correct the problems. It may be necessary to examine every aspect of the change process including goals, implementers, environment, attitude, skills, principles, and receptivity.

How Not to Do Change:
A Story That Should Never Be Played Out

In the fall of 1992, the superintendent of the Drecker City Schools attended a Tech Prep Kickoff Luncheon of the newly formed Drecker County Tech Prep Consortium to learn about this new concept in education he had never heard of before. The speaker at the luncheon was quite effective. The superintendent became so excited about the concept of Tech Prep that he picked up his car phone on the way back to his office to call a meeting with some of his senior-level administrators.

In the meeting, the superintendent expressed his enthusiasm for the Tech Prep initiative and his confidence that this was just the program that the community needed. "I think that this approach to curriculum and instruction will help our students who do not go to college," he said. "This is a low-income community, and we need to find ways to help these kids beyond high school."

He instructed some members of his staff to watch the video of the presentation on Tech Prep, attend a future meeting of the consortium, and report their plans for implementation for next fall. The staff was intrigued by the Tech Prep idea, but also a little nervous about this concept because it was unfamiliar to them. After viewing the two-hour video and attending another meeting on Tech Prep, they were even more confused—and overwhelmed at the far-reaching change that Tech Prep seemed to entail.

As the group discussed the meeting on the way back to the office, the Assistant Superintendent for Curriculum Development expressed his concern that this program would help only a few students and might limit their opportunities. "Surely the superintendent doesn't expect us to completely revamp our curriculum offerings just to track these students out of any opportunities for a baccalaureate degree!"

The Vocational Director who had been put in charge of Tech Prep planning at Drecker City Schools knew he was going to have to get the principal at one high school in the city to agree with him on piloting a Tech Prep program next fall. He visited each high school campus and met with the principal, but each one turned him down with the same answer: "I've got too much going on right now to try something like this; try me next year."

Finally the superintendent stepped in and "strongly encouraged" one principal to implement Tech Prep at his campus. As planning began for the fall, the campus principal, vice principal, and three district administrators worked on the changes for the coming year. They looked at other Tech Prep sites, studied the necessary curriculum changes, and spoke with an instructor at the community college. After drafting their secondary curriculum plans, they ran them by their district board, the community college, and the state agency.

Next, the principal asked one of the counselors at the high school to pull a group of students from class and speak with them about Tech Prep. A meeting was arranged for the parents, and a small group of students was enrolled before school let out for the summer.

In August, a selected group of teachers was called together and asked to participate in teaching a new applied curriculum. They were given the new textbooks and lab equipment and told to study the material in the next few weeks. Then the school year began, and the teachers, the students and administrators kicked off the "new vocational program." Somehow Tech Prep never survived.

This scenario presents a wonderful "how not to" picture for implementing any change, including a new Tech Prep initiative. A quick examination reveals some of the reasons this particular Tech Prep program failed to change the system:

- Instead of involving the implementers in solving the district's problems (with Tech Prep), the superintendent simply told his subordinates what would be done.

- Instead of being allowed to understand the problem and working through the solution, the implementers were simply handed the action plan and told to do the work.

- Only the top-level administrators felt any commitment and determination to put Tech Prep into play.

- The entire initiative was begun in an atmosphere of urgency and rush.

- Teachers were given little training and almost no time to prepare to teach the new classes.

The irony in this illustration is that the superintendent had every intention of doing the right thing. He wanted Tech Prep to be successful and was motivated to bring about implementation.

Without a plan and appropriate preparation, however, Tech Prep will never survive. Without knowing the principles and practices that are required of any change process, Tech Prep will never survive. Without a definitive plan that includes specific goals and action steps, Tech Prep will never survive.

Change That Works: A Story with a Happier Ending

Bob Krueger, Plant Manager of Pacific Graphics, the largest employer in Pleasantville, California, called his friend James Dunham, Superintendent of the Pleasantville Unified School District. Krueger was direct in this mission: "James, I would like to invite you and Joe (the president of Pleasantville Community College) to come with me to a meeting next week. Some of the area employers and educators have organized a partnership to work together in getting students prepared for work. Now, I know how busy you are, but these people are talking about something different, something new. I think it is worth a listen."

James thought a minute and responded, "Bob, this better not be another one of those 'programs.' If I tried to place another program in our high schools, the principals would hang me out to dry. We are trying to make lasting reforms in this school, and I have to work with my staff to make these reforms a success." The superintendent thought a minute more and then added, "I'll tell you what, Bob. If I can bring at least one of my principals with me to this meeting, I'll go."

"Sounds great! I'll send you dates, times, and some information about the meeting ahead of time."

The meeting turned out to be a worthwhile trip for all parties involved. They talked about the current problems in getting employees prepared for the workforce. The community college representatives complained about the fact that they did not have enough time with the students to teach them the advanced skills that the workplace required. The high schools complained about the unfocused and uninterested students who seemed to come and go through their system.

After two hours of hashing out problems, the president of the chamber of commerce introduced the superintendent of a school system in North Carolina, who talked about a concept called Tech Prep that was being adopted across the country. He explained the significant changes in curriculum and instruction that his district had made as a result of Tech Prep. He also talked about the improved performance of the students and the improved opportunities they found in the workplace. After his talk, as individuals began to ask questions and talk among themselves, an air of cautious excitement filled the room. Would it be possible to realize similar benefits in their community.

Those attending the meeting represented the key players who would be involved in organizing and implementing a Tech Prep consortium. They agreed to send a representative from each of their institutions as a team to North Carolina to review the site more carefully and interview other individuals involved in the planning and implementation of such an initiative. Then, after returning from the site, the consortium representatives organized themselves into several committees and laid out a plan of action.

No Tech Prep classes or curricula were put in place the next year. Instead, the time was taken up with detailed planning; thorough discussion; orientation of teachers, counselors, and employers; and initial promotion of the Tech Prep concept to parents and students. The Tech Prep planners and key players expected and received some resistance from selected teachers and administrators, but the reaction of the parents and students soon dispelled most of the negative comments and pulled down the barriers. When the school board saw the potential benefits for students and community, they were able to help in overcoming the resistance of the state education agency.

After a year of Tech Prep, community support was strong for the program; however, the need to cut all programs and refocus funding became an issue that had to be handled carefully. All individuals who had a potential stake in the cutting of these programs were asked to participate in a business/education committee meeting. Local employers discussed the needs of the business community, the jobs in highest demand, and the skills that would be needed to get those jobs done. After extensive discussion, the committee was able to come to a fair conclusion as how funds should be focused on curriculum reform in the next five to ten years. As old courses were phased out, new courses were phased in, and most of the faculty survived the changes that were taking place.

Tech Prep initiatives continue in the Pleasantville area, with consortium representatives orchestrating the changes that still need to be made in Tech Prep curriculum, instruction, and guidance. Tech Prep is still evolving in this community, but it is also solidly grounded in the secondary/postsecondary curriculum.

This second example of a changeover to Tech Prep in a local community presents a powerful contrast to the first example. Notice especially:

- the time taken to bring about effective change,

- the communication maintained throughout the process,

- the number of implementers included from the beginning of the process, and

- the logical, sequential, and thorough stages of implementation.

This is well-managed, effective change, and it can make a powerful difference for students and their parents, for educational institutions, for employers, and for communities. This is the kind of change that truly opens minds and opens doors.

Changes That Last

Remember the hula hoop, eight-track tapes, pet rocks? These were all innovations that enjoyed a brief popularity, then died away as quickly as they emerged. Then there were Coca Cola, pizza, salad bars, and personal computers. These initiatives took hold and grew in acceptance until they became part of daily life. The thing that makes an innovation persist until it becomes a systemic change is the perception that it has a beneficial use or fills a real need.

Public education is besieged with initiatives that promise to "put us back on top," and Tech Prep/Associate Degree is obviously one of them. But unlike some of the other initiatives, Tech Prep deserves to remain because it addresses a real need and offers significant benefits for the *majority* of our students. These include a chance to succeed in school, a more meaningful education experience, and better employment opportunities. But, to take its place among the initiatives that become part of the way we live, Tech Prep needs support, leadership, and commitment from key groups:

- Employers must be committed to the active support of Tech Prep both at the planning stages and in the classroom.

- Secondary and postsecondary teachers must be willing to change what and how they teach.

- Administrators and policymakers must be willing to commit the resources—by reallocating funds—to serve the neglected majority better.

- The community must be willing to support and encourage the Tech Prep/Associate Degree courses.

- Students—and parents—must recognize that good education (and good jobs) comes from recognizing that Tech Prep offers "something to use; something to build on."

When the minds of educators, employers, and community leaders have been opened to the changes that are required for effective education, the minds of poor-achieving students will be opened to useful knowledge and skills. When the doors of high schools, community colleges, and employer worksites are opened to provide the best learning experiences, the doors of opportunity for high-skills jobs—and high wages—will be opened for all students.

In 1993, more than 650,000 students in the United States enrolled in some form of a Tech Prep program. By the fall of 1995, that number is expected to grow to 2.5 million. And a program that has grown in one decade from a rudimentary idea to an enrollment of 2.5 million sounds like a major educational reform. Well, it might become one—and it would be a great one—but it hasn't happened yet.

Some very bold, significant initiatives for Tech Prep have occurred since 1985. Dale Parnell launched the reason for and the concept of Tech Prep in his book, *The Neglected Majority*. Pioneer educators created early, successful Tech Prep programs that served as models for others to emulate. Vocational education leaders teamed with academic leaders to create applied-academics courses in subjects such as mathematics, science, and communications to demonstrate ways for all students to learn. Policymakers such Congressman William Ford and Senator Claiborne Pell dared to take a giant step and push for Tech Prep funding in the Carl D. Perkins legislation—an action that has appropriated sixty to one hundred million dollars per year for states to create more than one thousand local Tech Prep consortia since 1991.

Equally significant is the fact that United States businesses, industries, and service organizations are in the process of restructuring the new American workforce. They are not only demanding the type of workers that Tech Prep provides, but they are also volunteering to participate actively in creating the programs and providing worksite learning experiences for Tech Prep

A CLOSING WORD

students. In fact, the 4+2 Tech Prep/Associate Degree curriculum structure has become a model for all school-to-work-transition education.

That's the good news. Once again, American ingenuity and the pioneer spirit has risen to create the solution to one of the greatest problems threatening our society in this century.

But the bad news is that Tech Prep as a true educational reform is still in its infancy. Many of today's Tech Prep practitioners have not caught the vision that is described in this book. They have not yet committed themselves to high academic expectations, integrated curricula, and contextual learning. Instead, many schools and colleges are just repackaging and renaming old programs under the Tech Prep label—and using Tech Prep funds to support their work. In these cases, many changes remain to be made, while old forms of turf protection and fear of systemic change slow down the process.

Meanwhile, another phenomenon is emerging. The notion of a Tech Prep type of career-oriented education is being recognized—and adopted— throughout the world:

- Tech Prep has been presented and discussed at two meetings of the International Vocational Education and Training Association (IVETA) meetings—the first in Thailand in 1992 and the second in Indonesia in 1993.

- Tech Prep and applied academics have been presented to three meetings of the Organization for Economic Cooperative Development (OECD): spring 1991 in the United States, fall 1991 in Switzerland, and summer 1992 in Portugal. During the 1992 meeting, a participant and representative of Germany asserted that "Applied academics and the Tech-Prep-type curriculum are the wave of the future for vocational education." In addition, Dr. Ron Tuck of the Scotland Department of Education presented a paper[1] advocating a new "general vocational education," which he said, "is called Tech Prep in the United States.

- Puerto Rico held a nationwide Tech Prep meeting in February 1993. Their schools have been teaching applied academics since fall 1992.

- Mexico's Ministry of Education is preparing thirty-five teachers to begin teaching Applied Mathematics in the fall of 1993. (The materials have been translated into Spanish.)

---

1. Dr. Ron Tuck, "Implementing Assessment, Certification, and Validation," a paper presented to the Organization for Economic Cooperative Development meeting in Portugal, summer 1992.

- The Chilean-North American Institute of Culture has organized and supported efforts in Chile to prepare fifteen Chilean teachers to begin piloting Applied Mathematics in the fall of 1993. The institute has sent these fifteen teachers and is planning to send ten Chilean local school administrators to travel to the United States for training in applied academics and Tech Prep, in addition to visits of Tech Prep sites in the United States.

- Canada is holding Tech Prep conferences and has a model Tech Prep/Associate Degree site operating in British Columbia. Three provinces (British Columbia, Alberta, and Ontario) have begun using applied academics.

Once, again, the United States has led the world in creating a new idea—as we did with the automobile, space exploration, semiconductor electronics, computers, biotechnology, and high-density television. Once again, other countries throughout the world have reorganized the value of our creation and are adopting it. Meanwhile, many educators and policy makers in the United States are dragging their feet about making Tech Prep/Associate Degree an integral part of our education system.

Currently we (the United States) are five to seven years ahead of the rest of the world in the development this education tool for creating a world-class workforce—a tool which can help us regain our economic edge. The question then becomes: Will we keep our lead, or will we give it away?

The United States is engaged in a major education reform movement aimed at providing continuity of learning and quality educational opportunities for all students. The Tech Prep/Associate Degree program, a significant element of this movement, focuses on providing meaningful educational and career preparation for the majority of high school students who do not complete baccalaureate degrees. In 1992, nearly one-half million young people were enrolled in Tech Prep/Associate Degree programs designed and developed through collaborative support and encouragement from communities, educators, and employers. Tech Prep programs challenge students and effectively prepare them to live and work in a highly technological society. These programs will provide the type of workforce our nation needs to compete once again in a global economy.

Combining secondary and postsecondary education programs through a formal articulation agreement, Tech Prep provides students with a nonduplicative sequence of progressive achievement leading to associate degrees in any of a number of technical and service careers. After completion of the strong academic and technical program in high school, Tech Prep students should be well prepared to continue their technical education at a two-year college to acquire an associate degree, enter full time employment in their chosen field, or pursue a baccalaureate degree at a four-year college.

APPENDIX

Tech Prep Associate Degree Concept Paper[1]

---

1. Organizational Affiliates of the National Tech Prep Network, *Tech Prep/Associate Degree Concept* Paper (Waco, TX: Center for Occupational Research and Development, 1992).

Why is Tech Prep Needed?

At a time when employers are demanding high performance in the American workforce, "more than half our young people leave school without the knowledge or foundation required to find and hold a job," according to a 1991 report from the U.S. Department of Labor. Today's workplace requires advanced technical skills and an ability to understand complex theories and processes in rapidly changing and emerging technologies. Most jobs that offer growth, challenge, and earning potential require a working knowledge of math, science, technical principles, and information/communications skills. Students well educated in the rigorous applied academics as well as technical skills can transfer their knowledge of principles, concepts, and technologies to practical applications in a variety of technical jobs.

What is Tech Prep?

Tech Prep is a sequence of study beginning in high school and continuing through at least two years of postsecondary occupational education. The program parallels the college prep course of study and presents an alternative to the "minimum-requirement diploma." It prepares students for high-skill technical occupations and allows either direct entry into the workplace after high school graduation or continuation of study which leads to an associate degree in a two-year college.

The Tech Prep program integrates academic and occupational subjects, placing heavy emphasis on articulation from secondary to postsecondary education. Articulation between high schools and two-year colleges embodies a competency-based, technical curriculum, designed jointly by business/labor and secondary/postsecondary schools, which teaches essential competencies without duplication or repetition. The advanced skills required to complete an associate degree at the postsecondary level in a chosen career build on the strong academic and technical foundation at the secondary level. The curricula currently being designed for Tech Prep/ Associate Degree programs will prepare better educated workers with advanced skills and the ability to transfer skills as technology changes.

Who benefits from Tech Prep programs?

American society and the economy will certainly benefit by the development of a world-class workforce which will enable American business to compete effectively in the world market. The cooperation at different levels of education will eliminate program duplication and provide greater efficiency in the development of human resources in our nation.

- Students enrolled in the programs are the big winners in Tech Prep. They develop strong academic competencies while obtaining a quality technical education. Even more important, they develop the competence and confidence to succeed in a fast-changing high-tech society.

- Employers benefit from the availability of better educated workers. The skilled worker shortages should be alleviated as Tech Prep programs become widely operational across the country.

- High schools benefit from implementing Tech Prep programs because more students have a reason to complete their education. The tone and morale of high schools will improve as more students engage in a purposeful and substantial educational program.

- Postsecondary institutions can raise the level of their programs to provide advanced skills because students will be better prepared for college-level courses. Spending less time and fewer resources on remedial or fundamental education programs, two-year colleges will be able to spend more on increasingly sophisticated technical programs, providing a foundation for continued learning and career development.

What characteristics do successful programs manifest?

A primary goal of Tech Prep focuses on learning outcomes achieved through multiple learning environments and teaching strategies which involve secondary and postsecondary institutions, business and labor, and government. Major features basic to the design and development of Tech Prep programs include:

Applied Academics

The context in which learning takes place includes not only the physical environment, but also the social/ cultural (values, relationships, etc.) environment as well as the internal perspective (learning styles, various intelligences, etc.) of the learners. The learning environment should be carefully designed and structured to enhance the meaning and usefulness of desired learner outcomes. Instruction must go beyond the presentation of theories and abstractions. The "whys" and "what fors" should be clear in the environment and examples in which students explore, discover, and incorporate the meaning and value of what is being learned into their own cognitive world.

The Tech Prep curriculum runs parallel to the college prep program in high schools, presenting a rigorous body of knowledge in a contextual setting and relating it to personal or social situations relevant to the workplace. Applied academics in mathematics, science, and communications form the strong academic foundation for the Tech Prep program which will enable students to understand complex technologies and new skill requirements in work environments. The program tolerates no "watered-down" courses but maintains the same academic integrity as the college prep curriculum, expanding occupational education to include academic development.

Applied academics courses address fundamental principles of productivity, teamwork, and flexibility needed in the workplace. Inclusion of applied academics in the Tech Prep curriculum provides the opportunity to build a solid foundation in fundamental courses in the early part of the high school program and to introduce the concepts of technology on that strong base. Because of the sound academic base, the student can advance to a specialty in the associate degree plan at a two-year college or seek a baccalaureate degree at a four-year college.

Local Partnerships

Employers, labor representatives, parents, and community organizations have equal representation with secondary and postsecondary sectors on Tech Prep councils or steering committees during program planning and implementation. The business/labor community identifies student outcomes required for future as well as current jobs; reviews curricula and course content for job relevance; and participates with educators to develop and provide work-based learning experiences such as shadowing, mentoring, cooperative learning, internships, apprenticeships, etc. Comprehensive and intensive partnerships must be developed and maintained between academic and occupational/technical education, secondary and postsecondary education, education and business/labor, and education and state/local government.

Articulation

Articulation is a process for coordinating the linking of two or more educational systems within a community to help students make a smooth transition from one level to another without experiencing delay, duplication of courses, or loss of credit. Educators from elementary, secondary, and postsecondary institutions will work together to design and deliver curricula with a continuity that facilitates steady progress from one level to the next.

Career Exploration and Counseling

Career awareness activities are essential for promoting Tech Prep/Associate Degree programs and recruiting students for the programs. This function involves a comprehensive, coordinated career counseling network of the facilities, programs, and skills of junior high/middle school, secondary, and postsecondary counseling professionals. To increase intelligent career choices, programs in career awareness, career exploration, and career/educational planning should begin at the elementary school level and continue throughout the college experience. The effort includes familiarizing students with many different job/career options, providing information on what is required to be successful in the positions, and leading students to discover and explore their own interests and aptitudes.

Associate and/or Baccalaureate Degree Potential

The fundamental courses prepare students thoroughly and proficiently for a variety of options after graduation from high school. Students may articulate into an associate degree program at a two-year college, seek a baccalaureate degree from a four-year college, or enter the workforce well prepared for an entry-level position in a chosen field, retaining the option to reenter career training later. The Tech Prep curriculum incorporates a series of exit/reentry points, each of which leads to a specific but progressively higher job classification.

Elevated Postsecondary Curriculum

The curricula of postsecondary institutions can be revised to an academic level consistent with expectations for college courses. Students entering college from a Tech Prep course of study in high school will be prepared to master advanced courses.

It may be several years before significant numbers of students will be graduating from secondary Tech Prep programs. Eighty percent of the people who will make up America's workforce in the year 2000 are already adults. Recent high school graduates as well as older adults in the community who desire to acquire associate degrees—the desired degree in many career fields in the future—may need preliminary academic assistance. A one-semester program, a "bridge program," includes academic foundation courses and some technical courses necessary to succeed in advanced associate degree programs. This program provides the essential elements contained in a high school Tech Prep program. A "bridge program" allows postsecondary schools to maintain or even raise the level of their course content to provide increasingly advanced skills.

What ensures a successful Tech Prep program?

Business/labor and government cooperate with education in a successful program. Employers who play an active role in the program can pique students' interest, help them form practical and realistic ideas about the work of work, and motivate them through awareness of career possibilities and expectations. Providing work-based learning opportunities that take students beyond the classroom will correct preconceived notions, erase misconceptions, and instill appropriate ideas about what is expected of them when they finish school.

In educational reform movements, teachers and principals are the ones who facilitate systemic changes at the foundation, thereby determining the degree of success of innovative programs. Teachers, principals, and counselors, as well as college faculty and administrators, must be included in all phases of planning and implementation of new Tech Prep programs. Appropriate inservice training and adequate resources will accommodate the achievement of Tech Prep goals effectively and efficiently.

The federal government has devoted significant funds to the support of Tech Prep through the Carl D. Perkins Vocational and Applied Technology Education Act of 1990. This support is accompanied by increased expectations for documenting the successful integration of occupational and academic learning. For continuing and long-term success, however, local resources must be reallocated to support the needs of the established Tech Prep programs.

The Tech Prep/Associate Degree concept offers an answer to America's mandate to improve our educational system and to remain competitive in the world market. A successful program promises to upgrade front line workers, improve the productive capacity of entry-level workers, and provide quality education for all students. With the cooperation, participation, and commitment from secondary and postsecondary educational establishments, local employers, teachers, parents, and students, the program will serve as an agent of positive change for the American workforce as well as the country's educational system.

This edition of the TPAD Concept Paper represents the contributions of a large number of leading Tech Prep practitioners and advocates. After review by many other researchers and educators, additional response to these insights will be provided. The National Tech Prep Network is grateful to all contributors of this important document, including:

Judy Kass
American Association for the
Advancement of Science

Jim McKenney and Lynn Barnett
American Association of Community
Colleges

Jim Kiser
American Counseling Association

Richard Miller
American Association of School
Administrators

Ken Chapman
American Chemical Society

Mary McCain and Joe Hudson
American Society for Training and
Development

Betty Krump and John McGrath
American Technical Education
Association

Bret Lovejoy
American Vocational Association

Helene Hodges
Association for Supervision and
Curriculum Development

Jill Scheldrup
Center for Workforce Preparation and
Quality Education

Arthur Doyle
The College Board

Tom Franklin and Terry Tabor
Council for the Great City Schools

Glenda Partee and Christopher Harris
Council of Chief State School Officers

Gary Moore
National Alliance of Business

Kathy DeFloria
National Association of Secondary
School Principals

Madeleine Hemmings
National Association of State Directors
for Vocational Technical Education
Consortium

Jerry Hayward
National Center for Research in
Vocational Education

Rebecca Douglas
National Network for Curriculum
Coordination in Vocational and
Technical Education

Jeremiah Ford
National School Boards Association

Larry McClure
Northwest Regional Educational
Laboratory

Gene Bottoms
Southern Regional Education Board

Harry Hajian
Community College of Rhode
Island/National Science Foundation

Ray Collings
Tri-County Technical College/National
Science Foundation

FURTHER READING

1. Berryman, Sue E. and Thomas Bailey. *The Double Helix of Education and the Economy*. New York: Institute on Education and the Economy, Columbia University, 1992.

2. Bottoms, Gene and Alice Presson. *Improving General and Vocational Education in the High Schools*. Atlanta: Southern Regional Education Board, 1989.

3. Bragg, Debra, et al. *Illinois Tech Prep Planning Strategies*. Springfield, IL: Curriculum Publications Clearinghouse, Western Illinois University, 1991.

4. Caine, Renate Nummela and Geoffrey Caine. *Making Connections: Teaching and the Human Brain*. Alexandria, VA: Association of Supervision and Curriculum Development, 1991.

5. Carnevale, Anthony Patrick. *America and the New Economy*. A report prepared for the United States Department of Labor. Washington: Government Printing Office, 1991.

6. Commission on the Skills of the American Workforce. *America's Choice: High Skills or Low Wages*. Rochester, NY: National Center on Education and the Economy, 1990.

7. Copple, Carol E., et al. *SCANS in the Schools*. A report prepared for the Secretary's Commission on Achieving Necessary Skills. Washington, DC: Pelavin Associates, Inc., 1992.

8. Dornsife, Carolyn. *Beyond Articulation: The Development of Tech Prep Programs*. A monograph prepared for the National Center for Research in Vocational Education. Berkeley: University of California, 1991.

9. *The Forgotten Half: Non-College Youth in America*. Washington, DC: Youth and America's Future: The William T. Grant Commission on Work, Family, and Citizenship, 1988.

10. Gardner, David P., et al. *A Nation at Risk: The Imperative for Educational Reform*. Report of the National Commission on Excellence in Education. Washington, DC: Government Printing Office, 1983.

11. Gardner, Howard. *Frames of Mind: The Theory of Multiple Intelligences*. New York: Basic Books, 1983.

12. Hamilton, Stephen F. *Apprenticeship for Adulthood: Preparing Youth for the Future*. New York: The Free Press, 1990.

13. Hull, Dan and Dale Parnell. *Tech Prep/Associate Degree: A Win/Win Experience*. Waco, TX: Center for Occupational Research and Development, 1991.

14. Kolb, David A. *Experiential Learning: Experience as the Source of Learning and Development*. New Jersey: Prentice Hall, 1984.

15. Parnell, Dale. *The Neglected Majority*. Washington, DC: Community College Press, 1985.

16. Secretary's Commission on Achieving Necessary Skills. *Learning a Living: A Blueprint for High Performance*. Washington, DC: Government Printing Office, 1992.

17. Secretary's Commission on Achieving Necessary Skills. *What Work Requires of Schools: A SCANS Report for America 2000*. Washington, DC: Government Printing Office, 1992.

18. Sternberg, R.J. *Intelligence Applied: Understanding and Increasing Your Intellectual Skills*. San Diego, CA: Harcourt, Brace, Jovanovich, 1986.

19. Thurow, Lester. *Head to Head: The Coming Economic Battle Among Japan, Europe, and America*. New York: William Morrow, 1992.

INDEX